A Celebration of Ministry

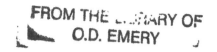
A Celebration of Ministry

Joseph Seaborn II

BAKER BOOK HOUSE
Grand Rapids, Michigan 49516

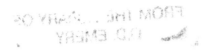

Contents

Acknowledgments

No matter how large our circle of friends, there is always a smaller inner circle of those who walk more closely with us along the lanes of life. It is their friendship which, in all of our celebrating, we relish the most.

For me, the inner circle of celebrants who added the optimistic tone to the following pages numbers about fifteen.

There are my colleagues in the Division of Religion: Duane and Wilbur, Richard and David, Malcolm and Keith, Judy and Neil, Leo, and Charles.

That fifteen also includes the office secretaries, Bonita and Janice, whose eloquence at the keyboard have helped turn this celebration into print.

And nearest of all is my family; Mary, who always sees the silver lining; Mary Joy, four, who has taught me to clap for small joys; and Joseph, two, who makes our home an outpost of heaven.

Only fifteen people. But apparently that's all you need on the inner circle to have unstopping joy.

Introduction

I Tend to a Garden

I tend to my garden. It is the most important garden in the world—the garden of souls.

Someone else took care of it before I came, and another shall tend it when I am gone. But for now the garden is solely in my care, so I tend to my garden.

I am often amazed at the beauty which God brings from the garden. There are orchids and roses nestled there that take the breath by their grandeur. Against the wall or under a thorny bush they grow. In one corner of the garden, away from the eyes of the crowd, a dozen lilies quietly scatter their breathless splendor.

Many of the flowers lack the nobility of the rose, but their presence adds fullness and life to the garden. Still others hardly show flower at all, but they bear delicious fruit.

Because the plants are so different they require all kinds of special attention. Several of them need to be watered daily. Others call for certain nutrients. For still others, no matter how scarce or abundant the rain, they always have enough.

Many of the plants in my garden are robust and vigorous. Unless I watch them closely and keep them pruned, they reach out and overgrow less lively plants, choking out growth by their sheer enthusiasm. Sometimes at the end of a long day, I vow that I am going to uproot a large section of slow-growing flowers and replace them with even more of the zesty type. But by morning light, I have reconfirmed to my heart the truth that the best and most beautiful gardens take time. *After all,* I tell myself, *perhaps it's not the garden that needs to be changed.*

A few of the flowers are so delicate that I worry from time to time whether they will survive at all. Every year—no matter how hard I try—I lose a few. For a while the garden looks sadly diminished. Barren spots sit around like plots of death; but I mark my grief, bring out the seeds, and replant in hope. It is my least-pleasant time but the whole plot is mine—so I tend to my garden.

I have noticed that the garden is always prettiest after a slow, gentle rain. As the fragrance of life rises out of the soil, the leaves glisten a richer green.

Every year I cultivate in hope that the fruit-bearing plants in the garden will bring a good yield, but I can never be sure about that. The changing seasons, the furtive rodents, the sensitive nature of the plants—all remind me that I must tend in prayer and leave the harvest with God.

Every now and then I bring in another gardener with special skills to help me improve my garden. And even though I ask his advice and usually follow it, I still work with my garden well aware that I alone am responsible for it. I know it better than anyone else. I know where it is vulnerable. I know where it is vital. Its beauty often fools outsiders into believing that it is completely healthy. But despite all the praise, I still take care.

Several of my friends have left their gardens unattended and, in time, weeds crowded in and turned a thing of beauty into a tangle of shame. I admit there are times when I get discouraged trying to keep it lovely all over. If I had a choice, I would stay near the fountain or under the archways, but I have to be careful about staying too long in a preferred spot, or else other parts of the garden suffer from neglect.

One of the happiest times of my day is when someone happens by and admires my garden. I like to visit and praise other gardens myself. There's something refreshing about visiting and enjoying other gardens. Many of them are larger and more ornamental than mine, but none of them ever fascinates me enough to keep me away from my own. I love my garden too well. I have grown with it. And when I can I want to be in it.

Few things in life compare with walking out in the garden and enjoying the steady growth that comes on day by day. Seedlings growing down and finding a firmer place to stand. Vines marching briskly up a wall. Buds slowly exploding into flowers. It's the kind of place where one would not be surprised to find God out walking again in the cool of the day.

Probably the garden would get along as well without my help, but I like to feel that I am making a difference here. And people who have watched me over the years give me an even better reason for staying. My garden is changing me too. One is nearer God's heart in a garden, so I tend to my garden.

Joseph Seaborn II

1

Resign or Re-Sign

Celebrating the Call

"If God calls you to be a preacher, don't stoop to be a king." When Charles Spurgeon made that statement a century ago, he summed up the feeling of most of us in the ministry: When it comes to sampling life at its zesty best, ministry is the place to be. If the best life is supposed to include love and scorn, high moments and low, poison and praise, you won't find any better vocation than ministry for tasting it all. Not only do you as pastor have to monitor your own highs and lows, successes and shortcomings, you also get paid to keep an eye out for how dozens of other people are doing as well. There they sit, scattered all in front of you every Sunday, with your being responsible for zeroing in on their needs and then saying twenty minutes' worth of something that will meet it.

In keeping an eye out for yourself and your people, you quickly discover two facts. One is that you yourself are most definitely human, a walking mass of impulsive motives. And the second is that your people suffer from the same malady. You give your best effort and they forget to say thanks. And you wince; or you go out of your way to keep the peace between a couple of hot-tempered people, and they still meet and blow up, and it's weeks before the explosion settles down.

And if it's not people who drain you, a chock-full schedule does. And if not the schedule, it's the pressure of decisions. And when the decisions are made, you wrestle with the consequences. Real ministry these days is hectic and draining with far fewer people cut out to handle it than we usually think. The person who quips that any old Tom, Dick, or Harry could cut it in the ministry hasn't been around it lately. Ministry today is no cakewalk. Most pastors today spend at least half of their time doing administrative tasks, or as one pastor dubbed it, "administrivia." When you add to that the need for keeping pace with moral shifts in society, the growing crowd of ethical issues that face our people, and the record number of options being offered for keeping a local church on track, it's no wonder that many pastors today are second guessing their call and bailing out of ministry in favor of more profitable pursuits.

In these days of candor, pastors too are more and more willing to say out loud that they are tired and discouraged with trying to buck the trends, that upstreaming in a downstream world is hard. There's too much to juggle, too many jobs to do to stay on top of it all, too much loss of image due to the scandals which have marred the headlines. You can hardly focus on pastoring for all the public embarrassment and management headaches you have to face.

How long the feeling lasts may vary, but all of us have felt it. You slump in a chair at the end of the day, vowing never to go back to the office again. Your mind staggers with overload. The muscles ache from hours of motion. Your body screams with fatigue. In the round of a single day you went from weary to worn to bushed—about as far down in the dumps as a person could go. You thumb around in the Bible trying to find that verse that says, "Be not dreary in well doing, for in due season you shall reap if you mope not." But you check both testaments and it's not there.

Your mind and body, long drained beyond usefulness, balked at giving out one more good idea or doing one more good deed. But you kept pushing. And instead of thinking positive and doing good, you slipped over into stinking thinking and half-hearted care. One pastor who got caught in that pattern said he would arrive at his church on Sunday morning so uptight that he dreaded to open the door, because it meant shaking hands with a bunch of people whom he honestly didn't love.

Most of us can remember with ease the day we grabbed our torch and set out to ignite the world for God. We felt unstoppable. Our note pads were piled high with truth which we knew without doubt would change the world. We were almost in the same orbit with God. A couple of lectures on evangelism had made it seem pretty simple; plus, with our zeal, what could possibly stand in our way? So we marched out and thrust in the flame but nothing burned. Those people who were supposed to be so eager to help us spread the gospel slammed doors in our faces. And the few who did agree to help us got off to such a halting start that we wondered at times if we should keep on trying at all.

As reality set in, we began to realize that our ministry would probably never circle the globe, that we would have to back away from our original plan of a convert per day. But we absorbed the shock of the setback and kept moving forward, convinced that though we were not marching nearly as briskly as we had hoped, at least we were going in the right direction. Only now we were advancing with a lot more wisdom about the actual size of our Judea. We had learned to select a spot considerably less than global in its dimensions and turn our energies to it.

In a way it's a great relief to be out from under that original global burden and under one that's more our size. It takes a lot of pressure off. The ego suffers a little, but at least we wear our hat a bit more comfortably. Plus now we have the added consolation that unless something goes terribly wrong, we can't make a global goof. If we mess up in managing our local acreage, we'll probably get at least one more chance somewhere else. Since we have decided against taking the whole world as our parish, at least we'll have another option if the first venture fails.

But even local ministries come with a load of frustrations. You mark it down and highlight it in yellow: *every ministry, no matter how large or small, can present the pastor with enough problems to sap all the joy out of his work.* A church of fifteen can cause migraines just as painful as a church of fifteen hundred. If people are not responding to the Word of God and moving together in unity, they are a pain in the neck to lead no matter how few and far apart they sit in the pews.

Some time ago I sat with a young pastor whose spirit was smothered with anxiety. He passed a handful of statistics across the desk to me.

"Look at this," he said, "I've been here five years and the numbers have dropped off every year. Every week somebody tells me I've got to start feeding the people, and pastor, I'm working myself to death and doing the best I can and I can't get this church to budge. I've tried evangelism, discipleship, children's programs—*everything*. Nothing works. I'm at the point where I can't even come up with a decent sermon. No inspiration. I'll be honest with you, I really don't care if I ever preach again."

That young pastor was facing what an alarming number of pastors are facing today. He was looking straight down the gun barrel of criticism. His personal pain was doubled because he was also having to live with the frustrating gap between what he knew his church could be and what it was. Instead of a church with its energies focused on growth and outreach, he faced a congregation in which inner tensions had all but suffocated him and stifled the mission of the church.

His predicament was echoed by another pastor. At fifty-six, this man was hardly your version of an amateur suffering from the greenhorn syndrome. He had been pastoring for thirty-three years and until now had met with fair success. But something happened. As soon as we fell into conversation, I knew that something had gone terribly wrong. A handful of disgruntled people had moved in against him with hostile fury and all but stifled his desire to share the Word at all. He had called on Friday to see if I could possibly arrange to come and preach for him, because as he put it, "I can't get a sermon to come. When I read the Bible, nothing happens. I feel cold and numb. If you could help me for just one Sunday, I'll try to come up with somebody else for next."

That Sunday morning he and I sat on the podium with 275 people gathered on the pews in front of us. As the song leader was directing the music, the young pastor leaned over and vented his hopelessness one more time. "They sure look like a dead bunch today. I doubt you'll even be able to wake them up."

Inside I groaned. Eighteen months before he and his wife had unloaded the moving van and taken charge of what they believed would be the pastorate of a lifetime. Every day for the first few months he hit the office in the morning, bursting with enthusiasm. Untapped opportunities lay all around him. He and his wife had celebrated their anniversary at the church by throwing an all-church party at the parsonage and giving their people a fifteen-minute speech on why they were glad to be among them.

Now here he sat, six months later, buried in gloom with roots of bitterness and resentment already growing in his soul. I wrestled to get the message out that morning. His dejected comments whispered just seconds before I stood to speak were weighing like lead in my soul. I felt out of balance, disoriented. Even as I struggled with the message, I guessed that my feelings of being smothered were only a fleeting hint of the terrible oppression that he fought against every time he stood in that same spot. If this was it, no wonder he couldn't find inspiration to preach. No wonder he handed his pulpit over to somebody else every time he got a chance. Even to stand before the people only pounded his spirit further into hopelessness. It was a vicious cycle and for a few moments that morning I felt it and hated it.

At lunch with him and his wife I lurched through a few bits of advice, but I drove home fully aware that two or three sentences of hope would barely make a dent on the surface of his need. Something more had to happen. Other larger answers needed to emerge.

Every person in the ministry knows the staggering mood swings that go along with managing and ministering to people. Not just from month to month as this pastor knew, but even from day to day and hour to hour. In the morning you pray over the body of a close friend killed in a car crash, and in the afternoon you visit the hospital to celebrate the birth of a firstborn son. One day you discover that the church is facing critical cash-flow problems, and your mind is thrown into a tailspin. The next week a person calls and wants to talk about giving a major gift to the church. On the way to meet the donor and describe your church's need, you daydream about how large the gift could be. On Sunday you preach your heart out, give the invitation, and no one comes forward. The next service you leave off the invitation, and two people come forward during the closing hymn. The frustration at the lack of a response of the past week gives way to the surprised gladness of the present glow. If mood swings were made to be criteria for fixing salaries, pastors would be among the highest paid professionals around. You go from dreary to cheery to weary and back again—and all within the course of a single day. Up and down. Glad and sad. On and on.

You sometimes run into the notion that a pastor ought not let his mood affect his work. At least not very much. It's the old idea that a professional should never give away his inner feelings, that he should always perform his work with poise and grace—no matter how delightful or difficult the circumstances. He should live in a mode of composure, sometimes even cool detachment. But for the pastor who really loves his people, that is impossible. He is called to identify with people, and when you identify, it drains off energy. You die a little at every funeral and get married again a little at every wedding. You hate family fights as you talk with a child who is torn apart by his parents' divorce. And you celebrate with a family who adopts two children orphaned by a suicide.

Maybe it would help if a pastor could know what was coming, if he could get a half-day headstart on the problems. But like the rest of life, ministry doesn't allow us to practice ahead. Whether we feel competent or shaky, it's ready or not, here we come. We get up to a brand-new day without the foggiest idea of the detours our schedule will have to take that day. We plan a morning of study, only to find that we have to hurry to the hospital to be with a grieving family, or we plan an afternoon for visitation and suddenly learn that we are expected to speak at a 7:00 P.M. function because the other speaker is sick. So we end up studying instead of visiting. Any person who enters the ministry, banking on a snug-tight schedule with every little detail having a neat preplanned slot and every issue coming with pharmacy-shelf neatness, is in for a shocker.

During my Sunday school days we had one teacher who was called the "Floater." This poor person was to be on standby for all the other teachers. If one of the regular teachers became ill or took a vacation, the floating teacher filled in. He often came to church on Sunday mornings and at the front door learned that seven junior-high boys were lurking in Room #4 waiting for him to enter the den.

The term *Floater* ought to be applied to every pastor. He has a schedule, but he has learned to sit loosely to it, refusing to feel guilty when all the items on the THINGS TO DO list aren't checked off at the end of the day, and all the calls which a demanding member wanted him to make are not made.

In order to cope with the steady stream of crises which seem to line up to get to you, you simply have to make a few firm decisions. The one that comes into focus in this book is that you in your ministry must decide what you will spend your time looking at. A lot of a pastor's confidence and effectiveness has to do with how well he balances his view of all that is happening in his church. It is as important, for example, for a pastor to remember that his people are not all bad as it is for him to remember that they are not all good. It may be impossible to always change your circumstances, but it is always possible to change your view. When it gets right down to it, the pastor has the noble privilege of deciding what he will focus on in the complex life of his church. He can choose whether he will spend more time curbing wrong or more time praising the right. No two pastors will ever approach the management of their church in the same way, but every pastor owes it to himself to choose his own view. He will do many things, but this one great step he must take—he must choose his own view.

He ought not let his enemies do that, nor even his superiors. The person who is called to guide a congregation must decide for himself about how he will image his people and his work. Once that decision is locked in place, the ups and downs of a single week will not shake him nearly so much. Two or three hot-headed members erupting on him at the end of a service won't bowl him over quite as quickly. Nor will he live at the mercy of praise, moping if he doesn't get one standing ovation after another. As he goes about his work from day to day, he will do so with the assurance that he is doing his best for God, and no matter what anyone says, lots of good things are happening around him. When friendships get shaky and dividing issues outnumber uniters two to one, he will stick closer to his balanced view, love his people, and trust God with the process.

Vision is a marvelous thing, but visions are decisions of the will. It's tough to keep a dream alive and well when most of the dollar signs in your budget are followed by rows of zeroes and the board is pitted against you like an angry nest of bees. Inspiration is wonderful stuff, and everybody ought to have some of it, but it's hard to be excited when you are being harassed by gossipmongers who slice away at your reputation every day. It's easy in times like that to get down on yourself and feel like Edmund in Eugene O'Neill's play *Long Day's Journey Into Night*. "It's a great mistake my being born a man; I would have been much more successful as a sea gull or a fish."

Ministers aren't kidding when they talk of troubles. It's the truth. Pick any ministry you want, and there will be enough problems in it to occasionally jerk the most optimistic person down off his toes. Ministries are few and far between that have no troublesome concerns stalking in the wings. More than likely, the best church you know about could be destroyed overnight if the right person made the wrong move. Even the best situation is fragile. Whether we know it or not, churches live on the brink. Something could go wrong at any time.

If you are going to survive in the ministry, you have to decide to see the good and give it a major portion of your time. Much of the spark of ministry is lost because we, being very human, focus too long on the problem and too little on the progress. It's so easy to glance at God and gaze at the Goliaths. Along comes a troublesome issue or a cantankerous person, and before we know it, we are zeroing in so intently on the problem that worry muscles in and closes off our view of the steady progress that is still passing us by on the other side.

Try It

Augustine noted that present fleas always seem worse than past diseases. Take a moment to test out his thought in your own ministry. To check it out, you need to bring two thoughts to mind. First, think about a major problem that you successfully dealt with sometime ago—a problem that is far enough behind you to no longer generate an emotional reaction when you think about it. Reflect on how you addressed it, and why you think it turned out for the good. Then think about a current problem you are facing. Take ne that's dominating your thoughts, even when you are supposed to be doing something else.

Compare the two problems; the one from some time back and the current one. How are they different? How are they alike? Is the present problem more serious than the past one? Does the nearness of it make it seem so? Or is the present crisis a "flea" when compared with the much more serious problem from the past? What did you do in the past that might help you better manage the current concern?

It took a surprising and unique message from God, but Bill finally came to realize that you have to choose your own view. A few years ago he hit rock bottom in his ministry. He had been pastor of his local church for five years with steady success. The numbers were on the grow. Year after year offerings kept climbing. The quality of Christian living among his people was on the rise. The church's reputation as an exciting, thriving congregation was spreading in the community.

And then it happened. Tensions sprang up about how to deal with the removal of a staff person. Nobody yelled or screamed, but subtle and powerful forces began to tear the unity apart. Attitudes were strained. The delicate nature of the situation was complicated even more because the person being released was the son of a prominent family in the church. Board members cornered Bill privately and attacked his handling of the problem. And in less than four months, the steady progress of five years had all but stopped. Bill's summary of his pain was sad, "I was as low as I had ever been in my life. There wasn't a day that went by but that my wife and I talked about resigning the church. There seemed to be no graceful way to back out. I didn't feel that I could say very much in front of my board because for several of them this was an intensely family matter. I was really in a bind. It went on that way for several weeks. Pressure. Bitterness. Sin.

"One day I remember sitting in my study feeling like a solid mass of discouragement. I didn't feel like opening a single book, not even the Bible. I didn't feel like doing anything. I really didn't care. I was just sitting, leaning back in my chair with my hands folded behind my head. Just to have something to do I glanced around the room, looking at the lines in the walls. My eyes fell on my ordination certificate hanging halfway down one wall. For several minutes I kept looking at it, wondering if I would ever have entered the ministry if I could have foreseen this terrible day. Without much purpose I got up from my chair, walked over to the certificate, and took it off the wall. I held it up close and looked at it. I read the words about gifts and graces and the confidence the district had placed in me. Then I looked at the signatures at the bottom. They were so faded that I could hardly make them out. I held the frame at an angle to the light, and still they were just barely visible. Without much thought I slipped the certificate out of the frame and out from behind the glass and walked over to my desk to look for a black-felt pen. Having found one, I began tracing over the three signatures so I could see them more clearly.

"As I was finishing the last stroke," said Bill, "a gentle impression formed in my mind.

"'About this church here, Bill,'" the Spirit seemed to say, "'you can either resign and give up, or you can do what you are doing to this certificate and re-sign. Resign or re-sign?'

"As I capped the lid back on the pen," said Bill, "a powerful surge of release swept through my mind—a cleansing rush of freedom leaped through my soul. I couldn't believe it. It was like having God himself suddenly stand beside me in the room. If I could ever claim that God spoke directly to me, that was it. I could either resign to the attacks of Satan and let a few members collapse the church around me, or I could re-sign, put my name back on the books as pastor and leader, and go back to my work in his power to start putting things back together.

"After the ink had finished drying, I replaced the glass

and frame and hung the certificate back on the wall. I had already made up my mind. I would definitely re-sign. For the first time in a long time I prayed with joy, 'God, for you I will trace over the same area again. I will not resign. I will go back to rebuilding again.' As I walked out of that office that day," Bill concluded, "I was a different man. The obstacles were still there. The despair still lay all around me. But I had gotten a new surge of confidence from God. I had gotten a new way of seeing my task. If God saw enough good in my situation to make a new start, I would too."

And he did. It took time, but over the years God was able to help Bill restore that ministry, remove the hostilities, and turn the church again into a tool for righteousness in the community.

For most of us the change from discouragement to new hope will not occur in a single afternoon in the study. Dramatic turnarounds of attitude are exceptions and not the rule. Even if we mustered all the optimism possible to our personality, we may still only jolt a part of our people into excitement. Those who claim that a church can change at the snap of the fingers are either one of two things: naive or shallow. They are either counting up changes that don't even exist, or else they are not really calling the people to radical discipleship.

In our power we can't always change things. If a few people choose to resist our leadership, we can't force them to follow us. If no matter how hard we work there is still only a smattering of growth, we can't take all the blame for that. People have free wills, and not all their choices are going to be good. No church is ever ravaged with such purity that sin never crosses the threshold. To lead people is to risk problems. But the pastor who pursues his work, aware of the bad without being glued to it, does himself a great favor: he gives himself the gift of a balanced view. When evil screams for attention and correction, the wise pastor will not avoid it, but neither will he worship it. He will give it due time, but he will soon be looking to the positive points once again.

There's too much worth applauding in our churches to let negative issues call all the shots. Every hardworking pastor has the right to celebrate. He has a right to turn his eyes to what is going right and, if necessary, mention it occasionally to the Chicken Littles who are sure that the sky above the church is falling in. The pastor with a balanced view always sees the good beyond the blatant bad. That's what leaders ought to do. They always see the silver lining in the cloud.

The pastor who preaches that his people must see the best in others must practice his own message. There will always be enough problems to prompt one to resign. But there will always be enough joys to inspire one to re-sign.

One way to break the habit of overfocusing on the bad is to go for a while overfocusing on the good. We may not change a single part of our situation, but we can work on our vision. We can make a decision to see and celebrate the good. If we can get into the habit of focusing on the good and true, we will give ourselves one of the greatest of all gifts—a discerning eye that sees the glory above the gloom. In pastoral work, both will always be present. But through the eye of faith, the pastor must make it a point to keep his eyes open to his whole work. As he does, he may be surprised at how large the good is when compared with the bad. Wasn't Augustine right when he laughed that our present fleas always seem worse than our past diseases? If the pastor can learn to celebrate his gains, the losses will more and more shrink down to the proper size. For the pastor it's a lesson worth regular review—his way of seeing will be his way of salvation. After all success in the ministry ought not be measured only by how many problems you solved; it ought to be judged by the number of situations that because you led well, never went wrong. They will never all be counted, but if they were, their number would be legion.

What you discover again and again in ministry is that you help your own heart by what you decide to see and what you decide to overlook. In ministry we have options about what we will let stay in front of our eyes and what we want to let go by the way. Every church will have a few people who try to bluff the pastor, but even bluffers have a virtue or two. As one pastor observed, "Every person has a reverse gear. If you push gently and long enough, everybody will back up. . . . " Thankfully God limits certain species in the churches, but never mistake it, they clearly are there. They may seem nearly untouchable in their hatred, but they are real human beings who need a pastor's care. Of course every church also has its gentle souls who adorn everything they touch. And the pastor who is struggling with the dark, surly side of church life needs to remind himself often that there is a lot about his church that he can celebrate, no matter how bleak things get at times. Even if your days at a particular church are numbered, you can still decide to go away pointing back to the good.

Here's the point. A lot of the joy and contentment in ministry is an inner decision of the will. When two or three features of church life take a downturn, we respond by turning time and energy their way. We zero in on the negative. Our perspective narrows to deal with the point of need. And in the process we lose sight of the positive that is still happening around us. Focused as we are for the moment on the dark side of the church's life, we are terribly tempted to mistake the dark part for the whole. Three miffed members can feel like thirty. A nasty divorce can make you feel like canceling the family. A broken furnace and two blown fuses can make it seem like the best thing to do would be to burn down the whole plant and start over. Two board members bickering causes you to wonder if it wouldn't be best to give everybody a gun and have them line up in a circle facing each other. Dark spots have a way of dominating the page. They throw off perspective. They cloud the eyes.

One antidote for overcoming the gloom of discouragement is to overdo our look at the good. As pastors we owe ourselves the benefit of a regular checkup in the matter of our perspective. As managers of people we can let 80 percent of our time be spent dealing with faults which come from about 20 percent of our people. When we do we are missing the fact that 80 percent of the church's life is moving along smoothly and growing quietly, but for the moment we can't see it.

Try It

As pastors we are often hesitant to applaud ourselves for successful work. It strikes us as self-promotional and probably is. But in our heart we know that there are times when we say to ourselves, *Hey, with God's help, I'm responsible for that going right. I did that and I'm proud of it!*

Take the past six months. As you trace back across your ministry for the past half-year, what belongs in a list of THINGS I ATTEMPTED THAT WORKED OUT PRETTY WELL? What belongs in a list of THINGS THAT I TRIED THAT DIED?

All success in ministry is partial. If you shoot for 100 percent, you'll likely, unless you are highly unusual, get about 50 to 60 percent of what you wanted. And frankly that's a typical success rate. If your lists are about equally long, you are probably meeting with reasonable success in your leadership and ministry. If you're achieving 70 to 80 percent or more of what you want to see done, that's called a *miracle*!

The chapters that follow highlight features of ministry that ought to be regularly in our line of sight. With all the possible aspects of your church's life that you might focus on, these stand out as steady sources of thrill and joy. To think about the positive points mentioned in the following chapters is no absolute guarantee of anything. You may be so discouraged that you honestly don't have in yourself the energy to redirect your mind. If the chapters that follow are linked with accountability and counsel from others, they may contribute to an overall pattern of restoration of joy.

When Moses raised a serpent on a stick, he knew very well that there were still plenty of snakes on the ground. The people were not to keep riveted to the ground in fear—they were to turn their eyes upward in faith. Their healing and help came as a result of what they were willing to see. Like them, we too can look and live.

2

Getting Tables Down the Mountain

Celebrating the Preaching Moment

If God keeps a video library of all the events in the Bible, there are two tapes that I want to see. One of them is the footage of Simon Peter as Jesus grabbed him by the hand to keep him from sinking in the sea. I want to see his expression both before and after. And I am curious to know how he got back to the boat. The other is Moses getting those tables filled with commandments down the mountain. I don't know how high he had to go on the mountain to get the commandments, but after God had finished writing, it was up to him to get the tables down.

Like pastors today he had to get the message of God down to the level of life. Tables (even tables written on by God) are no good until they make it down the mountain. Moses probably stumbled a time or two on his way down. A stump may have snagged his robe causing him to lurch and almost drop his precious cargo. A steep cliff may have forced him to take the long way around. It's all but certain that however he came, Moses had to do the job himself. No angel helped him. No divine conveyor belt dropped out of heaven to carry the commands while he walked calmly by their side. No. Moses carried the tables down by himself.

Wouldn't you like to have been watching as Moses began to inch his way down? Do you suppose he carried the tables for a while on his shoulders and then shifted them to his hip? Was he careful with them, or did he now and then slide them over a cliff into what looked like a soft pile of dirt below? Did he ever threaten to break them even before he got to the bottom because they were wearing calluses on his hands? We don't know. But when he finally looked out across the plain and saw his people and felt again their enormous need to have a message from God, all the strain must have been worth it. At least now he had done his part to make sure that the Word of God got safely to them. He had labored and lugged and sweated and now the responsibility of responding lay with them.

Sunday after Sunday, week after fast-moving week, pastors stand to deliver again the tables they have brought down from the mountain. It is a solemn task, brimming with its fair share of frustrations and questions. Grappling with a passage to draw out its full meaning is painstaking and risky work. If you are discouraged already, the work is all the more strenuous—the inspiration all the more missing. But when you have wrestled with it and are sure you have gotten from it what God would have you say, there are very few moments to compare with the powerful sense of satisfaction that you are hand delivering God's truth right to the heart of his people. No doubt about it, mountains make for treacherous and tiring climbing, but once you get to the valley and reach out with a timely truth, the strain of going up and back seems well worthwhile. The preaching task is no simple one, but anyone who does it for long will tell you that to be such a brief segment of time, it is one of the most thrilling and scary moments in a pastor's life. In the swirling world of ministry it is a moment of extraordinary grandeur.

Very few times in ministry pulsate with so much energy as the moments before the message when you once again stand at the foot of the precipice with treasure from the world above. At the same time you experience both a high and a low, a thrill and a burden. The rising energy so necessary if a sermon is to spring to life is at the same time invigorating and yet difficult to manage. There's a mounting inner confidence, but there is also a tinge of nervousness that expresses itself in a very practical way—you need to visit the restroom.

You welcome any little distraction as a way for getting a moment's relief from the inner tension. You pick at a fuzzball on your pants, or thumb through your notes one more time to see if they have moved since you stuck them in your Bible. (Usually they haven't.) You glance to make sure the pulpit is free of books and clutter and swallow again at that thick sensation in the back of your throat. If you have enemies in the audience, they stand out like flashing lights on a police car.

No wonder preachers often say that they are drained at the end of the morning message. What the people see is only a small part of what is really going on. In terms of stamina requirements, the preaching moment is a whole category unto itself. Nothing quite ranks with it for sheer exhilaration. But nothing quite compares with it either as a time when the pastor hopes the people can't see all the turbulence surging in his soul. In part the rising fervor traces to a fact which every pastor knows: very few moments in ministry rate with preaching for having the potential for either helping him soar so high or else dive so deathly low. One pastor who had known his share of down times after preaching put it this way.

> I used to go through mini-depressions every Monday. From early in my ministry, I felt compelled to preach the world's greatest sermon every Sunday. And frankly for me I found that was all but impossible. So I hit upon another plan. Now I study hard and work at improving, and when I have done my best, I trust the Spirit of God to make it fruitful beyond my human abilities.

If I feel that I have done poorly, two lines keep me going. One is, "Okay, God, if you don't do something to help them hear and apply this message, we've got problems." And the other is, "Hey, God. Sorry, that was pathetic. But please, God, give me one more shot at it. At least give me one more Sunday."

Try It

The next time you preach a real loser of a sermon, one that drops on the floor right in front of the pulpit and doesn't even make the first row of pews, try this: Wait three months and have another go at the same subject in a slightly different way. See if you can carry it off the second time around.

It is amazing how strongly we feel about how well or how poorly a sermon went. What to us may have been a colossal flop may have been to another person a new set of wings for soaring. Knowing that another person was helped helps a little, but if we feel badly about a sermon, no amount of compliments can take away the mood. But give that a try. Wait three months and present the same subject and see what happens. Usually you will find that it wasn't the subject, but your own tiredness or discouragement or frustration that colored your feelings about the message.

When the second sermon is finished, compare your feelings about the two. Which one felt better? Why is that? Do you find that, like the rest of us, your personal mood or your mental agenda at the time of delivery plays an enormous role in your overall reaction to the sermon? Do you give yourself a second chance to salvage the sermon without coming down too hard on yourself for the first attempt? Why not take Dave's advice and at the end of a message that missed, instead of saying, "That's not a subject I can handle," say, "Okay, God, give me one more shot. All I want is one more time."

As you sit on the platform waiting to preach, you are always keenly aware of the number of items in the order of worship yet to go before you speak. You find yourself guessing about how long the next prayer will take, the next song. As you mentally check off each item you find your spirit pulsing with a larger and larger build-up of eagerness. Half of it is anticipation, sheer excitement about one more grand time to talk to your people about God and his interest in their lives. The other half is anxiety. Will you say the right thing? Will you say it well? Do you really have the Spirit's leading in the message? Will you land anywhere near where your people are living right now? Will someone go away offended?

You want to stand with confidence and preach with boldness, but one side of your emerging feelings makes you wonder if you should even stand at all. You will be talking about truth that existed long before you were born and will be around long after you have died. Most of what you will say the people have heard before. A few of the congregation, in fact, will probably know more than you do about the subject. You will be more reminding than informing them. So you toy with the feeling that maybe you should keep your seat and just let the organist play another majestic piece on the organ.

As a pastor I have often wished that my body would remain more calm during those final few moments before I stand to deliver God's Word. I almost feel that it would help me to get the message across better if I could reason my way along the path of the sermon, coolly assuring my people of the eternal truth which is now within their grasp. Perhaps if what I was about to say didn't matter so much, I might be able to approach it with steadier nerves. But the words which I plan to say deal in the circles of life and death, so I accept the heavier responsibility that truth in that league deserves and hang tough. I take a firmer grip on the arm of my pulpit chair and wonder if the people on the front pews can see that my knuckles are a shade whiter. I smile a little inside when I realize that in a few moments, as God's Spirit directs, many of the people in front of me will be holding on to their seats with conflicting energies flowing in their hearts as well. At least that is what I pray will happen. I pray that at least some of the powerful forces that are at work in me will get out beyond the podium and into the hearts of those who need to feel them the most. I pray that those who sit way in the back, trying to stay aloof and poker-faced will feel so deeply what I am feeling that they will have to leave quickly if they plan to hide what is happening in their souls.

The special song which precedes the message begins, and you feel like a parachutist moving toward the gaping door of a plane at fourteen thousand feet. Slowly you are moving toward the time to make the leap. You have done it a thousand times, but every jump carries its own risks and rushes. You can never tell when you step to the pulpit whether this will be a disappointing venture or a soaring, lofty accomplishment. Will you sit down at the end of it with a feeling of futility? Or will you look back from where you came and say that all in all the experience left you exhilarated and refreshed? You never know, but as the time draws closer to stand, you begin to think less about the outcome and concentrate more on the event. You hear the strains of the organ fade with the soloist's voice and for that one split second you pause again to tell God one more time that you are standing for him. You don't want anybody to miss that. You rise from the chair, nod to the soloist, and approach one of the holiest places that a human being will ever know. As you open the Bible, a hand larger than the hand of your father (and more gentle than the hand of your mother) seems to wrap around your shoulders and with the sudden infusion of a higher power, you take the leap and begin to feel the winds of another world sweep past your soul. As you fall you pray only that others will feel the winds as well. It is a magnificent moment, splendid with the presence of God. A lot of moments in life are awesome, but to have the chance to live a high and noble moment every week is one of the rare and lofty privileges of pastoring that never ceases to broaden the soul.

During the delivery of the sermon, the preacher stands on the brink. Sitting all out in front of him are people whose attention is in constant flutter. At any one time several of them are being distracted by a crying baby. Another two or three are dozing off. A mother is planning her noon meal. Two boys are playing "Connect the Dots." If we knew the truth, there are probably points in the sermon when less than half the attenders are genuinely listening. On the other hand, we would be encouraged if we knew how many people who look like they aren't even present are really absorbing our words at a deeper level than even we are intending.

Anyone who preaches will always continue to be struck by two factors. One is the stunner of what people think you said. You aimed in direction *A*, and someone is convinced you were preaching right in their direction, and they live at *B*. A thirty-year-old mother met me down the hall after worship one morning and said, "Pastor, that was just what I needed today. I've been having trouble lately in my attitude toward my husband and that message helped me deal with that. I just wanted to tell you how much it helped."

Naturally I thanked her. But as I walked on down the hall, I thought, *I didn't say anything even remotely close to dealing with attitudes! I distinctly remember that my sermon was about getting a global vision for the lost.* I didn't have the heart to go back and ask her how her husband got into a sermon on world missions. Instead I decided to credit the Spirit for once again taking words which looked more natural draped around one subject and custom fitting them around another.

The other feedback that takes us by surprise is the one in which a person whom we thought never did get into the flow of the service—much less the sermon—picked up precisely what we were trying to say. I have observed dozens of people in a worship service whom I was sure, even though they were present, were still not there. But at the end they smacked me wide awake with their insight into what I had tried to say.

We need a reminder now and then that how we feel at the end of a sermon is not always in accord with the facts.

We've been taught to mistrust feelings when it comes to salvation. We should learn to lean loosely on them in sermonizing as well. What may be a blunder to us may well be a boost to another. God keeps the correlation off just enough to make sure that we always remember that the results are mostly his —that whatever happens is far greater than our blotch or master stroke could ever cause by itself.

No matter how much or how little of our sermon takes on any given Sunday, preaching is still a privilege. Every week from all across the community people gather voluntarily to hear us read and explain the Word of God. Most of them will drop something in the offering just before we speak. If they were looking for entertainment, they could possibly get off more cheaply—and probably get better quality—elsewhere. But they come. The stockpile of chores around their homes argues against them even leaving the house at all. Playing catch-up alone could take up their whole day. But still they come and sit and wait. They block out half their morning once every seven days and trust us to fill it. It is true in part that they come out of habit—but a habit without a measure of reward soon dies. They must have a stronger reason than habit that keeps them coming. The likely fact is, they keep coming because they get help. Somewhere in the songs and prayers and in the words we frame, they find hope.

They could go elsewhere. But they don't. They come and sit down in front of us fully aware that we are as human as they are. But that makes them even readier to listen. If we have lived in the real world and tried out the truths that we are about to proclaim, perhaps they will be able to use them as well. So they come because they need to hear what we have to say. They believe that what we will say will help them face up to life. They give us the better part of an hour to tell them how life can be better because they live it by God's Word. That's an honor. They will give us a combined total of many hours of their time in hope that we can fill them with worthwhile truth. They want to be different when they leave at the end of the service. And in more cases than not they are.

Not every sermon is a cliff-hanger. Many of them in fact are more like cliff dwellers, up there somewhere and having a hard time reaching the ground. But frankly congregations aren't usually built up by a bunch of cliff-hangers. The pastor who trains his people to believe that every service will be a cliff-hanger and that every Sunday needs to see the bulletin chucked in favor of a dose of high-octane emotion is in trouble. God is a God of order and that ought to be reflected in some degree in every worship experience. A steady proclamation of the Word of God accompanied by a living response by our people may not bring out the news media nor win a preaching prize, but it is the surest way for growing healthy and disciplined people.

For five years a pastor in a nearby city had a "Super Surprise" for his people every Sunday. He would bring in a knock-'em-dead singing group or a wow-'em speaker or have a puppet show or a celebrity testimony service. He became known as Rev. Fad, always after the hottest thing, or wooing the latest craze. Every week the Saturday paper advertised for people to come see the "Super Surprise" this Sunday. As long as he stayed, the idea seemed to work pretty well. The numbers grew and his church was the talk of the town. Almost everybody and his brother visited the church at least once to check out the thrill of having Rev. Fad unveil his "Super Surprise." Even I went once.

But when his successor decided to return to Bible teaching and prayer and leave the surprises in the box, the attendance dropped by half and public attention quickly fell away. Many began to doubt the depth of the previous approach for building up believers in the ways and Word of God.

Steady exposition of the Bible week after week may not call out drum rolls and congregational confetti, but the joy of ministry ought not lie in drums and parties anyway.

They are too fleeting and fickle. What gives more joy is the steady (although sometimes zigzag) growth that you see quietly and gently coming into the lives of people as you feed them the solid Word sermon after sermon. One pastor put it well.

> I enjoy the rush that I feel when, in grappling with a sermon, suddenly God gives me the perfect illustration or outline to carry the truth home. I love making the Scripture leap off the page and come alive to my congregation. I love to help people experience God's Word, not simply hear it. When that happens, I feel I have done exactly what God first called me to do.

If the pastor had only the satisfaction of seeing his people grow in God as a result of his preaching, it would be enough. But there is more. Even during his own sermon, right in the middle of his own thirty marvelous minutes, he can make it a point to learn and grow as well. The joy of helping others get a better grip on God's Word feels good. But the pastor who wants to maximize the preaching moment will also, along with his people, want to take in and learn from what he is saying. The old cliché makes two points: "Keep your index finger pointed at the people, but keep your thumb (and all the rest of your fingers) pointed at yourself." If we as pastors make the effort during our sermon, we can see and absorb new insights into our own soul.

Every preacher knows the experience of preaching along and having another completely unrelated thought pass through his mind. When that happens, it means that our brain is moving faster than our mouth and in its spare time it's staying busy. With a bit of practice the pastor can train his brain. In the split seconds it has while it waits for the words to catch up, he can train his mind to reflect on the sermon itself, on how his people are responding to him, or on how he can grow from his words himself. Written out verbatim, such a sequence of thought might run like this:

SPOKEN WORD: "God is always working at the point of our pain."

INNER WORD: *Boy, am I glad that is true for these people. Jill and Bob really need to hear that today.*

SPOKEN WORD: "He always knows exactly how and precisely when to apply his healing touch in our lives."

INNER WORD: *Thank you, Lord, that this week you had my father call and apologize for his rude attitude at the dinner.*

SPOKEN WORD: "No one is ever outside the range of his care. It reaches as wide and as far as any human being can ever go."

INNER WORD: *A few years ago I would have wondered about that when I first met Tom. He had gone about as far into habitual sin as a person could go. Personally I thought he was hopeless.*

SPOKEN WORD: "Do you ever struggle to believe that God really cares?"

INNER WORD: *Help me Lord, to listen closely right here in these next few moments. I'm about to say something that I myself need desperately to hear.*

When looked at this way, the sermon becomes a sandwich with public proclamation wedged in between bits of prayer and praise. It creates an amen corner in the soul. Without ever missing a verbal beat, you let the antiphony of praise and proclamation be the silent and spoken partners in your mind. You enjoy the inner echo of truth as it vibrates again far more personally in your own heart.

Try It

Once you consciously try it, you'll find that it's not a distraction at all, but a way in fact to sharpen the focus of your sermon. Most of us talk inwardly to ourselves as we preach anyway. We do it because the brain has time left over while our words are still catching up with our thoughts. We can think far faster than we can talk, so our thoughts move into reflection on what is still flowing through our lips.

If we can get into a habit of applying the truth ever so briefly to our life and experience, we will wind up speaking more clearly because we will speak in terms of actual living—ours! Without ever making actual public personal reference we can be in the constant process of testing our message against the reality of our own life. If it fits there, it will probably fit into the lives of others. If it seems artificial and unrealistic to us, it will probably strike other people that way too.

As you preach there is another wonderful truth to keep in mind—the truth you are proclaiming belongs to the whole congregation. As one pastor phrased it, "Preaching is a two-way treat." You stand up on Sunday, hoping to accurately reflect the Word of God, but what you also know is that no one person's word is the final word on *God's* Word. All of your people are helping the truth to happen. A few of them may even be hindering it from happening. But what that means is *that you are not finally responsible for their orthodoxy or lack of it.* They have to decide their own patterns of belief. You can only point clearly in one direction. They do not need to use your vocabulary to know your Lord. And that is at once a tremendous relief and a majestic hope. As one pastor observed, "When I speak to a man about Christ, an unseen energy within him reinforces my words. I have an ally in every man I meet. There's a God-shaped void in every life."

Sometimes on Sunday as I sit on the platform, I worry that I won't be able to get my message all the way out to the people, especially to those sitting slumped in the back pews. To deal with the frustration of distance, I often imagine that I have a large lasso which is easily able to loop around the farthest seat. With the help of God I am going to toss it far enough to corral even the most distant person and draw him into the power of the gospel. The image genuinely helps. When I stand, I am not nearly so bothered by people sitting light years away. I have convinced myself that the distance is not one of yards but one of mind-set.

As the worship progresses, the people may not move bodily, but I fully expect that in spirit they will shift a dozen pews closer. By the time I finish the sermon I hope that in attitude no one will be sitting on the back pew.

For that to happen, the message must soar with power and land with relevance. Making it soar is the Spirit's part. Making sure it says something that links with life is ours. Our purpose in preaching is to package truth so well that it's easy to get a lock-tight grip on. A roll of insulation and a gallon of paint may weigh about the same, but they are not equally easy to haul up a ladder. The bulkiness and lack of a handle on the insulation can make even the carrier look incredibly clumsy.

People rarely carry long what they cannot carry easily. If they leave worship services with no good place to get a grip on what we said, we may get to the exit and find a stack of sermon pieces lying at the door, assuming they are solid enough to stack. But give a sermon a good mental handle, and it will not only be carted out the door, it may also get passed around in the marketplace and get repreached, although surely never quite as well as at the first. In more ways than one, your sermon ought to be the talk of the town. When you hear someone somewhere referring to something you said long ago, there is a sudden rush of joy that rises to remind you that your labor is never in vain in the Lord. Not every sermon rings the bell, but when God touches your work with his anointing, a lot more gets accomplished than you usually know.

When we preach well, we don't need a sign that says: PLEASE SIT UP AND TAKE NOTICE. The sermon will say that itself. As a pastor you have the privilege of deciding how long you want your people to remember the life principles you are teaching. You do that by casting your message in a memory-locking form. One of the most frustrating and disappointing words to the ears of a pastor is to hear one of his parishioners quoting another speaker from six months ago who said exactly what you said last Sunday. No question about it, it causes a letdown. But the cure for that is not resentment, but a promise to work at saying truth more vividly yourself. As your picture of the truth is more focused and attractive, they will begin hanging it more prominently on the memory walls of their minds. And like the little yellow signs so common in car windows, they will begin hanging a tiny sign on the window of their soul that reads: DOER ON BOARD.

It is possible, you know, to wrap orthodoxy in a package so ugly that it's not only resented but frankly sneered at. "It sounded good," somebody will say, "wonder what he meant by it?" Generic packaging may be okay for groceries and drugs, but in sermon making it is strictly taboo. No matter what words you wrap around truth, you will always crush it a little in the process. So why not promise to go ahead and make it pretty while you're at it. Letting it go forth bluntly and ugly is no virtue. Dress it up and let it march out with grandeur and class.

If we labor under the notion that our way of putting truth is the only way to do it, we miss much of the joy of preaching. We become so weighed down with the burden of believing for others that we forget that they have a part to play too. Truth also belongs on their shoulders. In fact when pastors get too pontifical, too certain of their local infallibility, God usually brings along a lesson which helps them renounce their omniscience and rejoin the human race.

Recently my friend Dave got a traumatic reminder that he was still very much fallible. Three men in his church devised a crude, cruel scheme to test his sense of humor. For three consecutive Sundays they would go at him, one at a time, and raise questions about the declining quality of his sermons. According to plan, at the close of the following Sunday worship, one of the men swooped in for the kill.

"Hey, Pastor, that's all right. You can't have a good sermon every Sunday. We're praying for you, and God is able."

"Up to that point," said Dave, "I thought I had done

pretty well. But his comment jarred me. I went home blue before Monday."

The following Sunday another accomplice met him at the door after the sermon.

"Psst, Pastor. Come over here a second. Hey, Pastor, I hope you don't feel bad about today's sermon. You've had pretty good ones in the past. I'm sure you'll get it back. We're behind you."

"Man, you talk about being down in the dumps," said Dave, "I was really struggling now. I racked my brain trying to figure out what I had lost. Whatever it was must have been pretty serious. In any case, I moped home even lower than I had been the previous Sunday."

"My wife, however, was beginning to have a hunch."

"I bet those guys are trying to pull your leg."

"Maybe so, but if they are, they're getting up closer to my chest."

The next Sunday I took her advice and waited for another assailant to show. Sure enough, here he came.

"Pastor, thanks for your message today. I learned a lot from the two or three parts I could understand. Sometimes quality is a little tough to come by."

"No, not really," I retorted, "I'm just trying to match my sermons to the quality of you guys' humor." My wife was right. Those guys had pulled my leg, but, boy, they had nearly pulled it off.

"On the way home," said Dave, "I felt another emotion—relief. I was sure happy that those guys had been joking. That prank could have devastated me. My sense of humor survived but that was one 'joke' I could have done without. I thanked the Lord that at least for the duration of their stunt, they had probably been listening closer than at any other time. The next Sunday I went back to my pulpit with a brighter glint in my eye and a sigh of relief that God had restored unto me the joy of presentation."

When Moses first reached the valley, he probably wished that his people were only pulling a prank. There must have been an instant when he wished that he had stayed at the top. Even though he had only been gone a few days, the people had already begun dabbling in sin and indulging their fatal fantasies. When he smashed the tables, he was only venting the same emotion that we as pastors feel when we do our very best to lead our people in the way of life only to have them bellyflop in the cesspools of sin. Today we wouldn't throw a table at them. But we are often tempted to hit them with our Bibles. On days like that we need to decide again to take the long view. If Moses could have only seen how those ten statements would, over time, mold the value system of not only his people but that of a major portion of the world, he would not have been so quick to dash them to pieces. In the short run, sin seemed so widespread that any hope of turning the people toward God looked downright silly. But Moses climbed the mountain again; he went to the podium one more time.

And in the end the tables, which had seemed so small against such great odds, wound up transforming an entire society and a crowd of other cultures beyond. It took a generation and more but it happened. Our work behind the podium may on any single Sunday seem futile, but we need to stick to it and keep rejoicing because when God is in it, the word can still move mountains.

3

The World on the Potter's Wheel

Celebrating Insights into Truth

When the message first flashed across his mind, Jeremiah must have guessed that he was getting a miscue. He had already seen it. In fact, he had seen it that week. No use going down there again. But the more he argued out of logic, the stronger the signal, "Jeremiah, I want you to go down to the potter's house. I want to show you something."

"But I've seen that guy work, God. He's good, but he's not that good. Is it really worth another trip?"

"Yes, I have a special message waiting for you down there."

"Oh, I see. Okay." And Jeremiah was off.

He had gotten used to God doing that. Taking a scene that he had seen a hundred times and overlaying it with a new coat of surprise colors. In fact when a commonplace event which he had seen a ton of times suddenly exploded with a rainbow of truth-soaked insights, he had come to take that as a signal that God was speaking. So in spite of the fact that he had watched the potter before, and knew him by name, and had even bought several of his creations, he made a beeline for the house. God had promised to meet him there, and Jeremiah had practiced the presence of God enough to know that the potter's house would be alive with revelation today. So down he went.

No sooner had he taken up his stand near the wheel than God turned on the creative energy. Every movement began to vibrate with truth. The potter shifts his feet. "God, what do you mean by that?" The potter dabs at the rim of the vessel. "What's he doing now, God?" A chip of clay falls to the floor. "God, do you mean anything by that?" Then a major mar. "Oh, God, I can see that by myself. I know what you have in mind with that. Israel's like that, isn't she, God?" By this time Jeremiah is one solid sensor. The event is erupting with truth and his mind is working feverishly to take it all in.

The slow-turning wheel. The flecks of dross. The gentle hands. The hunched shoulders. Remakes. Scraps. Every facet of the picture seems to rival the others for a turn in the mind. And one by one Jeremiah soaked them up and savored their significance.

As he moved from point to point in the picture, he could hardly believe that he had never seen it that way before. Clay that stood for people. Hands that seemed like God's. Fragments thrown back as if to get a second chance. It was a marvelous sight; God's by-line was showing up at every stop of his eyes.

The potter must have been puzzled at Jeremiah's comment as he walked away.

"Hey, man, thanks. Wow, you've given me enough sermon ideas to last a year."

"Say what? I gave you what? Where's a sermon?"

On the way home Jeremiah's mind must have been in a whirl. Sermon ideas churning out in every direction. Even titles were already filtering to the front. At least three Sunday sermons were ready: "The Pot That Never Boiled"; "As the Wheel Turns"; and "Working with a Bunch of Lumps." He could just hear his people now as they read down through the bulletin and hit those titles. "Pretty blunt title. It looks like he's gonna be coming straight at us today." And they were right. Jeremiah had gotten some mighty strong words from God and he was known for passing them along uncensored. But that's also what they admired about Jeremiah. They knew he had gotten his signals directly from God. He would not be echoing what he thought some other prophet had claimed that God said. Jeremiah had gone down to the potter's house for himself. The details in his sermon were clear and sharp and fresh. The pictures he painted sparkled with recent life—regular and robust life. And they listened all the more closely because when Jeremiah spoke, they sensed that he and God had been together. The stuff he talked about was straight out of life, but it had the signature of God scrawled all across the side. The message was clear because it resonated with daily living; it was true because it came from God.

Potter wheels aren't very common today, but God still keeps his prophets on the lookout. All across the landscape of our lives there is an unlimited supply of pictures that pulse with all the energy that Jeremiah found in the rotating wheel. Layer after new layer of rich truths lie about us like manna waiting for a new harvest every day.

Like Jeremiah we will occasionally receive messages which have a tone of sternness and require us to shoot straight from the hip. Not every sermon is meant to salve. Some are meant to sear. And like Jeremiah there will be times when we preach out of sheer determination and not out of inspiration. Anyone who says that every sermon comes complete with a supply of glad anointing has simply missed the gate and hit the fence! When you are discouraged with your congregation and your mood has lingered down below the misery line for days and even weeks, you are hard put to come up with a sermon that soars to the heavens and lands on the clouds. And frankly not all sermons should. When Jeremiah finished preaching that day, the ideas were excellent; the tone was tough. But both he and his people knew that he had spoken, not out of happy optimism, but out of blunt realism, and the message hit sharply home.

One of the clearest confirmations of the call to Christian service is the fact that God is constantly helping our minds pick up clues to truth and life in the wide world around us. By the power of his Holy Spirit he brings together our attention and some brand-new idea and bonds them together as permanent partners to pass along as a new duet to the memories of our people. Instead of seeing just a dolly full of tools hoisted high by a crane to prevent thievery, we see a parable of the human soul held aloft by God to keep it safe from Satan's greedy hands. Instead of seeing only a set of steps leading to the second floor, we see a picture of a soul gradually ascending the hill toward God. And we turn the stairway into a prayerway of thanks. More than a chef trying to get the sticky dough off his hands, we see a person trying to rid himself of a tenacious nasty habit.

Sometimes in our low moments we forget that such insights are not commonplace for people. Part of God's call involves creative vision, and we are often privileged to have it in ways that would surprise our people if they could suddenly see what we see.

Almost every new glimpse of our eyes provides another image for transporting truth to the minds of our people. It is our privilege to work in a world where the whole environment is crammed with objects that we can mentally melt down and reshape into building blocks for the soul. Everything we see is a potential partner of a truth. Every event is an insight waiting to happen. As pastors we thrill to the fact that a part of our work is not only to convert truth into life, but also to convert life into truth. In linking the realm of the body and the realm of the soul, we are constantly shuttling back and forth and trying to train our people to do the same. But we must never chide them too severely if they are not able to match our level of performance. After all it is part of our unique call that God adds the special ability to see more than what is quickly visible.

For the pastor who works to take fuller and fuller advantage of this ability, there simply is not space in a Sunday-morning sermon to put all the insights that accumulate in his mind over the course of a week. Most of us usually force an illustration or two because we found something that just won't wait. But all of us have had the pleasure of seeing more than we are ever able to say. We have to resort to the fine art of blot in order to squeeze it all into thirty or forty minutes. But we leave the pulpit satisfied that there is much more where that came from. We may have said a lot, and even too much for one time, but we did not nearly empty our minds of everything we know on the subject. There is always more—much more. And all because we, like Jeremiah, have had the joy of letting God open a score of new windows on his world.

One of the most magnificent gifts which God gives to those whom he calls to his service is bilevel thinking. Most people possess this gift in measure; the preacher enjoys it to a high degree. James chided his readers for having a double mind, but a double mind is exactly what a pastor wants. Almost every day of his life he is in search of truth in the daily round. His thinking can regularly move in the bilevel mode. He sees with the optic nerve, but he also sees with another nerve that reaches to the soul.

There's a fascinating and puzzling combination of words in 1 John 1:1 which at first glance is confusing. But on closer scrutiny, they bring this factor of bilevel thinking clearly into focus. As John begins his description of Christ, he uses terms back-to-back which on the surface seem redundant. In John's words, "That which was from the beginning, which we have heard, which we have seen with our eyes, which we have looked at and our hands have touched—this we proclaim concerning the Word of life." Notice the phrases, "which we have seen with our eyes," and "which we have looked at." They seem to say the same thing. But closer inspection opens an insight. When John referred to seeing with his eyes, he had in mind visual perception, what happened through the iris and retina and pupil. He had seen Jesus in person.

When he added the term "looked at" he had in mind a deeper vision. He had lived with Jesus long enough to see his purpose—the mission that brought him to this world. He had looked deeply into Jesus' very heart, and when he put the visual view and the inward insight together, he was drawing as close to divine wisdom as the human mind will ever come.

In a similar way the pastor sees and perceives. Through the miracle of eyesight he takes in all the panorama of scenes and shades around him. But he does much more. He looks at them long enough to let their deeper meaning emerge. What to another person may remain only a surface look becomes for him the very stuff of his trade—truth embedded in life.

At a recent conference, I stepped to a window to get a breath of fresh air. A note on the window seal caught my eye. It read:

> Be careful about this window. It's no problem to open, but closing it is a pain in the neck. Thank you. Maintenance department.

Immediately I copied it down. My mind had raced off to James 3 and the terse warning there about the tongue. That note would fit well at the window of the mouth too. It's easy to get it open, but shutting it can be a pain in the neck! I could never have guessed that an illustration that would help me deal with a couple of my people would be waiting in the window. But I offered thanks to God for the Maintenance Department and filed the idea away for the message to come.

For the pastor the whole world is a study. We don't have to be sitting in a chair in an office to do our work and do it well. Our study is a large room with the sky for its ceiling and the clouds for shelves. If we are stuck in the middle of an eternal traffic jam, we are in the perfect spot to stop and look and listen to people under pressure. Including ourselves! In five minutes we can observe enough horns blaring and hand signals that have nothing to do with turning and necks craning and doors slamming and vocal chords straining to write a fair-sized illustration book of our own. Or we can walk down by the lake and watch a six-year-old drown worms, while his father sits calmly by wondering how a fish can bite a hook which, 90 percent of the time, is dangling above the water. No picture is safe from our discerning eye. Every object within visual range becomes a potential packet of truth waiting to be opened.

One of the reasons that the pastor can grow to be more patient than many other people is that he is always in the right place at the right time to work his trade: the observation and interpretation of life. Every road he drives along is on the map of insights. Every phone call he makes is a possible link with a lesson. Every single minute is brimming with a pregnant point. The books that occupy the shelf are really the smaller section of our library. Without having to shell out a single dollar, we have constant access to the largest library in the world—the world. And the book is always open. Not only is it open, the pages are always turning by themselves.

One of the greatest frustrations of my ministry has been unnecessary interruptions—people who needed to rattle on about nothing special but who were convinced that they were talking substantive stuff. I think every church must come complete with at least one interruption specialist. If you let it, that can get under your skin. One of the worst of this breed is the intruder who plies his trade whimsically. There you are glued to a task that you've been trying to finish for days. You've got papers spread out all over your desk. You need about thirty minutes, and thirty minutes is about how long you have before you need to leave for the hospital. If you keep to the pencil, you can make it. You can almost feel the end now. The desk will be tidy in twenty-five minutes. The project will be neatly folded and placed in the drawer and that marvelous feeling of closure will spread across your soul like the smell of piping-hot bread fresh from the oven.

And then the secretary calls.

"Yes?"

"Pastor, John is here." And you talk about jerking a flesh hook in the heart. That does it. You have heard John's name so many times that the very sound of it sets off a series of sirens in the soul. And all of them are red and glaring and loud.

"Pastor, John has just walked in and says he needs to see you right now. He says he only needs to ask you one short question. He says it will only take a second. Can I tell him you'll be right out?"

Pastors should not bite telephones, but for a moment that emerges as the option of preference. "Just a second" is the most regular lie that pastors ever hear. And even if it were just a second, you are so agitated now that you couldn't finish the project anyway. So out you go, leaving the oh-so-close project and praying that all he wants is five dollars for gas. Maybe you can do the handout routine and be right back.

But the moment you step out to shake his hand and try to smile and he motions for you to sit down, you can go ahead and hang up the project and possibly the hospital as well.

"Pa-a-a-a-astor." When John starts out that way, it's going to be a *long* few minutes. "Pa-a-a-a-astor, I've been having a little problem lately."

"I'm sorry, John," you try to sound concerned. "What's bothering you?"

"Pa-a-a-a-astor, you'll probably think I'm a little silly coming all the way over here to talk to you like this. [He's right about one thing.] But, Pastor, I've been having trouble hearing your sermons lately and I was wondering what people would think if I started sitting down closer to the pulpit? What do you think, Pastor?"

And you thought biting a telephone was bad! For fifteen eternal minutes you push every ounce of graciousness you can find to the front of your face. But if John goes on much longer, he's going to run the risk of hearing where you'd really like him to sit. But like God you remain slow to anger and plenteous in mercy. And when John finally ambles to a conclusion full of gratitude for your amazing insights you are a basket case in need of the hospital yourself. The seven-fold thank-you which he compiles that caps off his departure is the ultimate irritation. If it didn't sound so pious, you'd close with a word of your own. But you only nod and shudder and glance in the direction of your secretary who smiles that soft and subtle smile that lets you know she thoroughly enjoyed it.

Have you ever wondered if people in your congregation ever ask themselves if they interrupted you? Did you know that it is likely that there are still people in our congregations who really believe that we sit in our offices all day long, hand over the receiver, waiting for them to call? Thankfully God limits the species. But there are enough of them to keep your schedule slightly out of balance. But mark it down: we will always have a few people in our care who rank right up there with Job's comforters and Nehemiah's critics as the classic carriers of senseless palaver.

But take another look at John's visit. On the surface it was a blowout, a totally useless waste of two grown men's time. By nearly every criteria you can think of, it got off to a bad start, continued in a foolish way, and closed with absolutely nothing accomplished. If every act of ministry had a similar purpose and met with similar stunning results, we would have to measure our progress in negative numbers.

A few days later I went back and gave that debacle a second look. I had cooled off enough to look at it for its deeper insights. Here's what I came up with. In less than twenty minutes, John had helped me in several areas.

1. I had practiced the delicate art of graciousness even while a far less noble virtue was stalking in my soul.

Every pastor needs to keep in practice with graciousness.

2. I had learned again that people and not projects are what the church is all about. A project will never be in heaven—but John will. (I hope God does not assign me to help him find a seat!)

3. I had modeled a decent spirit in front of a secretary who, next to my wife, sees her pastor at his blatant worst and best.

4. I had taken a giant step forward toward my goal of being more patient.

5. And, I had collected a marvelous illustration on interruptions which would come in handy in the future. The truth is, concerning people like John, we growl about them at the time and gloat about them when it's over. The good news about a story like John's is that you can use it to top almost any other story. And when it comes to stories, every preacher needs at least one tall tale that is really true. He needs one great story where he can speak "evangelistically" and deep in his heart know that he is right on target. Fortunately most of us have more.

Try It

Bring to mind the most recent incident you can think of which really got under your skin. Perhaps it was a confrontation with someone, or a traffic snarl, or a disagreement with your spouse. But think of something that raised your emotional temperature. At the time you felt so angry and frustrated that you couldn't have gone straight to the pulpit for anything. If you had, you would have belched and bellowed nothing but an ugly attitude.

But if your feelings have settled down about it, go back to it and salvage the insights. As you look at it now, what practical points can you draw out of it that might help you and others the next time a similar thing occurs? As it was going on, what did you do right? What would you like to be able to do over? What have you changed about your beliefs or your behavior as a result of that incident? Can you identify one specific way you have improved as a result of it?

It is this commitment to turn all of life, even the awkward incidents and confrontational moments, into stepping-stones for spiritual growth that is the goal of living. If you share your insights with your people, one negative experience might well have a multitude of positive results.

There is no other vocation in all the world that is so able to use so much of life for its resource. Every little moment is bursting with possible clues for seeing truth more clearly. Every conversation is a living book filled with reams of crisp one-liners and new turns of thought. Walk through a clothing store, drive along a freeway, visit the hospital, and truth is sitting at every corner just waiting to step up and introduce itself. It may take practice to discover that the best illustrations are not in the book *701 Outdated Illustrations for Preachers,* but if we can stay with the practice, the insights will come. Some of the best illustrations that will ever get into our sermons are sitting around in your day like land mines waiting to be triggered by a searching mind.

Once you set your bilevel thinking in motion in a steady search for truth in the common round, you will discover the delight that far from running short on ideas Sunday after Sunday, you run long. You wind up having to sift out perfectly good material because Sunday morning sermons are not supposed to exceed half an hour. But as one pastor put it, "I'd much rather have to squeeze than to stretch."

Sometimes when our minds are tired and overextended from the daily grind of giving and going, it is hard to be stimulated even by ready-made material in a outline book. But perhaps an active search in a new direction, outside the study, might be just the step for opening up both new insights and a new place for finding them. Occasionally our minds need to be pushed out of hiding and exposed to the incredible detail that marks this gigantic world. For a lump of clay so large, it is amazingly detailed in its crafting. Ordinarily the larger an object, the less little things count. But when God built the universe he went for both size and specifics.

What is thrilling is that we only see the first two or three layers. Many many more, known only to God, must lie beneath. Just as there must be hundreds of caverns tunneling beneath the earth which have not yet made it to the tourists' maps, so God's truth is so deep and so thoroughly meshed with his creation that a perpetual explorer could never see it all. It would be like trying to see the Smithsonian in a day or playing Bach on a pitch pipe. The tool is not up to the task.

During my childhood I did something that caused me enormous agony—I grew teeth. There was a time in my young life before girls came along that I genuinely questioned the wisdom of growing teeth. The only possible benefit I could see from it was that it gave dentists a way to make a living. So in spite of the fact that I harbored a consistent distaste for dentists, my mother still made it a point to invite me to join her on frequent visits to his chair.

On one visit, I came across the only valid reason I have ever found for going to the dentist's office. While sitting in the waiting room, I pulled from the shelf a magazine called *Highlights for Children*. I had never seen the magazine before, but, did it ever get my mind off the chair and the drill and the needle. Especially the page entitled "Hidden Pictures." There on one side of the page was a series of hidden pictures to look for and across the page was a larger picture loaded with details including the dozen hidden pictures. There was a rake, a duck, a thimble, a hat, a book, a flower, and more. So I picked out one of the items and started scanning the picture page with all the commitment of a diver searching for sunken treasure. If I couldn't find the item with the picture right side up, I'd flip it upside down. Or sideways. It might be on the housetop or in the tree trunk, but I'd hang tough and grab mother's arm when I made another discovery. I don't know who invented "Hidden Pictures," but he ought to win the

Nobel Peace Prize for helping children face a dreaded dentist.

For the pastor, "Hidden Pictures" is the title across the page of life. We have to look at more than what first shows up on the surface, but if we hang tough, there are hidden truths enough to fill a lifetime of sermons with pure gold. Once we get in the habit of seeing the second layer of realities, it is a daily joy to see just how often a scene opens up a deeper message.

Try It

In an upcoming sermon make it a point to only use illustrations that have come from your own observations of life. Don't open a single illustration book for once and force yourself to see illustrations of the truth that you are trying to communicate hidden in a picture down the road, or in a tree, or on a building, or in a conversation. Pick the five or six places where your outline needs an illustration and go off in search of five fresh ones that didn't first pass through another person's mind.

If you go the extra mile to make them fit with your people's exact experiences and mention a specific story or a specific intersection or (if it's complimentary) a specific businessman in town, you will ring the bell even more clearly. But for once do all your illustrating from scratch and listen to your people's reaction and see how you feel.

When we see and seize a metaphor from the daily round, we quickly discover that even a metaphor is no dead thing. Jeremiah saw the sudden mar. It was an ugly hole, but it soon flooded with meaning. Even the scrap from the scar formed a new lump of clay. And that glowed with meaning too.

An insight is a squirming lively thing. It will rarely lie still for more than a few seconds of observation before it mutates and grows a limb or adds a section or flips completely over. No behavior lies outside its bounds. It dances and cavorts and somersaults and reshapes and redefines itself at the edge of the mind, taking on complexity as it comes nearer the center.

In 1 Corinthians 2:12, 13, Paul uses a phrase that takes the whole of this chapter and squeezes it into a half-dozen marvelous words.

> We have not received the spirit of the world but the Spirit who is from God, that we may understand what God has freely given us. This is what we speak, not in words taught us by human wisdom but in words taught by the Spirit, expressing spiritual truths in spiritual words.

Look at his meaning. The term "expressing" which Paul uses here was a term often used by shoppers down at the local clothing market. Just as people do today, it was not uncommon for people of Paul's day to carry with them to the clothing store a shred of cloth from a piece of clothing in order to match the colors. If a lady had a beautiful toga dyed with the deep purple of the murex mollusk, she might even take the whole toga to the market to compare its color with that of a shawl. Only by careful comparison in the light could she be sure of a perfect match.

The best way to get that exact match was to lay the shred or a garment against several other garments. Perhaps five or six colors would be close, but only one would be a perfect color match.

In gleaning insights, Paul had done the same thing. He had felt inspired by God with a great truth that he needed to communicate. And instead of putting down his own words or even the words of another person, he had held a range of vocabulary alongside the great truths of God, allowing him to help Paul choose just the right terms to get the point precisely across. He had compared spiritual ideas with spiritual words. If God helped his mind to move toward a specific picture or an exact term, that was the one Paul chose.

As pastors we are not writing the Bible, but we are engaged in the same divine task. We are always in search of a picture or a pattern that will exactly communicate God's grand truths. We have a whole assortment of God's truths always pulsing in our hearts and often pounding on our minds. What we do for our people is to hold up pictures and ways of seeing that truth so that God can help us find exactly the right vocabulary vehicles in order to get that truth all the way to our people. We compare insights from the Scriptures with sights from our world. When we discover an image that is helpful as a carrying case for an insight, we rush off to our people to tell them all that we have seen and heard.

Sure, we will jettison a lot of ideas, but never the first time they turn over in our minds. Once is not enough to have a clear sense of their worth and wonder. They might be like just another baby in a manger, until we look long enough to see the angels hovering nearby, and hear the shepherds saying something about the Son of God.

Ideas may be as delicate as a daisy or as enduring as a rock—but never underestimate their power. Words have a way of standing people up and marching them forward. Sunday after Sunday we have the high privilege of advancing people in the most holy faith by the sheer power of anointed words. We may at times get discouraged with the level of their response, but we must never forget that if we have walked with God, and if we have seen his signature etched on his world during the course of the week, and if we can point to it in front of our people, we have accomplished our part of the task. We have, like Jeremiah, just gotten back from the potter's house with ideas so fresh that the wheel is still spinning. And when we speak, we have the assurance that we have done our best to speak clearly and currently for God.

4

The People Came Together

Celebrating People in Worship

By anybody's standard, it was a massive undertaking. Hundreds of thousands of people needed guidance from one hostile environment to another. The tyrants of Egypt had been ruthless, and the people were thrilled to get away from that bastion of hatred. But the Canaanites were no angels either. They hardly lined up to form a welcoming committee when they looked across the Jordan and saw the Israelites encamped on the other side.

And the desert stood as the enemy in the middle. The Egyptians were grueling and the Canaanites inhospitable and the burning desert was only more of the same. At both ends and in the middle, the conditions were bad. Any one of the three would have been cause enough for a perpetual complaint, but all three together only heightened the tension. Points for unrest and potential explosion stood as thick as parking meters along a main street. And Moses knew it. He knew that the people had very few options, which made the climate always ripe for massive rebellion. Except for a miracle from God, there was no hope. And so Moses at every junction of the journey did the wisest thing a leader could ever do. He drew his people together to have them look to God. He built a tabernacle of worship, and every time the tension mounted he turned to the tabernacle and to the cloud and to their God.

He couldn't very well change the surroundings; he could only point his people beyond it. He could not alter the terrain, but he certainly could alter the gaze, and as often as he could, he did. He would stand at the door of the tabernacle and turn to glance at the faces of his people. As far as his eyes could see they were standing in the door of their tents, with their eyes and hearts fixed upon God's glory in the cloud.

Moses was not naive. He knew that many of the people standing in the tent doors had murmured against him. He knew that a few of them had always hated to eat quail, and they certainly didn't clap when God put it permanently on the menu. He had to come down hard on a few of them because they had violated God's laws. He was well aware that they were still smarting from that. He knew all too well that a good number of the people standing behind him, if they could vote, would put *no* on the ballot.

And with all the energies pulling at the people and all the range of their attitudes toward him, he knew he could be their leader only if on a regular basis he gathered them together to remind them that they were in this thing together, and that God and not he was finally in control. The very fact that we even know of an Exodus today is due in large part to the fact that all along the way Moses gathered the people and gave them to God. They were God's people, and if they were ever to make it safely into a new homeland, it would only be as they played down their differences and played up their unity and walked as one people with God.

There's a reason why Sunday mornings are special to pastors. Sunday mornings are the one time in the week when our people get together as one body to look beyond themselves to God. The rigors of the week have drained them physically and mentally. Their schedules have been clogged up with more events than one human being ought to tackle. Many of them have given and gone and guided until they themselves have slipped over into a weary low. If worship had no higher purpose than to pool their burdens and weariness, it would be a miserable merger indeed.

It is however far more than that. It is a chance for them to elevate their days to a higher plain of purpose; an opportunity to see the glory above the gloom; to walk for a while in the realm where God lives and to see the tapestry from the other side.

Pastoral work is a string of surprises. If you wrote down everything you did from Monday morning through Sunday night, it would read like an article edited by a paper shredder. The dozen tasks you worked at on a Tuesday afternoon alone would be enough to baffle the brain.

For all the taxing work of the week, Sunday morning makes it worth the while. The people may have mixed feelings about you as they gather, but at least for a time they sit quietly and hold their peace. They may not all be worshiping and a few may even be scheming, but at least Sunday is God's time to talk, and when he's in the company, they dare not butt in. So on Sunday mornings the people come together and the week converges into one point. Our people have made a thousand steps and walked a thousand ways and said a thousand words, but on Sunday morning they gather from near and far and stop their walking and talking for a while to hear from God.

Sunday morning is the rest of the week all rolled up into one. It gathers up the scattered snapshots of the congregation over the past seven days and presents the week in review. Right in the same service sits the man who called to complain about the bathrooms, and the couple that just got married, and the man who is running around on his wife, and the lady who won the Teacher of the Year Award that week at the local high school.

As Pastor Roy stated, "When I go to the platform on

Sunday morning and look out over the congregation, I see faces of people that I have been able to walk with through some special or difficult experience. Sometimes it is the loss of a loved one, an emergency call in the middle of the night, or a special request for counsel when their world seems to be falling apart. Maybe it's a wedding, a baby dedication, a spiritual victory at the altar, a time of laughter in their home or ours, or their testimony at a crossroad in their life. I find myself sensing a special love and appreciation for the flock and offering thanks to God for the victories."

As pastor you know an amazing amount of what your people did during the course of the week. Most of them have no idea how often their stories get back to you as pastor. Not all the stories are good. Not all are bad. But on Sunday the people and their unique stories get together to become the grand story of redemption on a local scale.

If love covers a multitude of sins, the pastor is a great lover. Every Sunday morning he stands before a group of people about whom he knows a lot more than they would ever guess. In fact if some of them really knew how much he knew, they'd probably stop coming. They'd be too embarrassed. But he stands before them knowing their sins as well as their strengths.

He knows that one of his Sunday school teachers has a hot temper, that he yells at his wife and children almost every day. He knows that the man sitting on the fifth pew from the back is getting too close to a secretary in his office. Already as pastor he is working on a strategy for dealing with the problem. When the moment of truth finally comes, the man may be angry. He may be repentant. The pastor doesn't know for sure. But he knows that he needs to face him. It's among his hardest tasks, but as a caring pastor he has no option.

He also knows that the two young ladies who sit in the back left corner have made a covenant between them that once a week they will do a good deed for someone who could never pay them back. They have asked that their work remain anonymous to the congregation. A dozen thank-you notes on file in the church office and two new members in the congregation remind him that their work is very well known to God.

More than anyone else in the church, the pastor knows his people. Just one glance around a group on Sunday morning and he can spot the gossipers and the gripers, the helpers and the lookers. He knows who calls him most on the phone and who prefers to come and take his time in person. He knows who stays on the fringes and whose vote counts for more than one.

It's surprising that the pastor isn't the biggest gossiper in the church. He could be. He could put half the gossip columnists in his town out of business in just one spicy article. But he clamps his lips and believes the best and holds his peace. He stands in front of a hundred juicy stories every week but refuses to let a single one of them slip out to less-caring minds. He cannot forget them, but he dare not divulge them.

The stories stay in his memory for a reason. They remind him that his people are still within Satan's reach. The tug of war is real. If God and good are to triumph, it will mean sealed lips and steady prayer and deep belief.

And the pastor does believe in his people. In large part he believes in them because they also believe in him. Sunday after Sunday they come and sit on the pews in front of him and wait for a word from God. Even though a few of them are struggling in Satan's grasp, they believe their pastor is right; there is only one God in the world. The power of evil may be strong, but it is limited. It's potent—but it's tied. There are not two gods out there competing for their souls. God alone has all power. And while they may be grappling in the grip of sin, they need to hear their pastor say it again, "God alone is victor. He alone is all powerful. He alone will prevail. He alone forgives and heals."

The caring pastor always thinks of his people in precisely that light. They may be losing here and there in their battle against sin, but God is on their side, and they need to hear that. They can win. They can triumph. The pastor believes that strongly, firmly, deeply.

When it comes to pastoring people, the language of the decade is much more appropriate than the language of the hour. While it is true that major spiritual redirection can occur in a moment, most of it happens step-by-step over a long stretch of years. Those who have a need to measure the impact of their influence every few days would be poor candidates for the pastorate. In spite of all the reports we fill out, the fact is that ministry doesn't readily lend itself to easy analysis. Even in churches that experience sudden numerical growth, there is need to be cautious about hasty tabulations because numbers are amazingly unreliable when it comes to measuring true spiritual growth.

Try It

Get out your membership list and examine it using Nature of Spiritual Progress as your criterion. Divide it into three groups. First go down the list looking for the people who made a sudden and sure about-face in life—people who were clearly unchristian who suddenly in a leap of faith came to Christ and never wavered once in their commitment. At least as far as you know, they never toyed with the idea of turning back to their former lifestyle. Then second, identify the people on the list who are clearly Christian but whose steps at first were wobbly, their loyalty to Christ and the church shaky. Perhaps they reflected that by spasmodic church attendance or occasional spiritual mess-ups or even flagrant sin. You have no question now about their dedication to God, but in the beginning you or a previous pastor wondered if they would stick with it long enough to become a stable Christian. Then look at the other people on the list and see if they are the ones who are still on the periphery. You aren't sure if they have reached a point of undivided loyalty to Christ. They still need encouragement and coaxing and love. Unless your church is highly unusual, the second and third lists will be longer than the first. But the very fact that the second group is so large is cause for hope. In this matter of faith, stability and steady growth often follow a period of immaturity in which you as pastor can only watch and pray.

Every pastor celebrates when the numbers climb. But wise pastors celebrate with care. They know that early spiritual steps can be mighty slippery and halting. All of us have seen churches in which a charismatic leader ran up a large number on a tote board, only to leave and send the church into a tailspin. It is very likely that if Christ walked into our churches today, he wouldn't even glance at that RECORD board still mounted on nails in the corner of the sanctuary. Numbers are such fickle indicators of anything that they often mislead more than they fairly represent.

To say that a church of fifty is weak or a church of a thousand is strong without knowing more of the circumstances is like saying that the only great river is the Mississippi and that the only real delta is the Nile. The fact is, without several other less-famous rivers, there would not be a need to mention the size of the Mississippi and the Nile.

I suppose if God had wanted to, he could have invented a religion that didn't need for its followers to meet together. He could have designed a faith that would only thrive in solitary confinement. But he didn't. He made the kind that calls for getting together from time to time. Apparently there is something that God planted in the human heart that works best when it is refined in the company of others. It must be a vacuum of sorts that can only be filled by belonging to a gathered group. Whatever it is, it is a marvelous urge to watch.

On Sunday morning you can stand in the foyer of your church or on the side of the sanctuary and the low drone of language fills your ears. These unique people who have been apart all week, walking the ways of work and play, stand around in groups of three or four or more, catching each other up and networking all their lives into one grand story. It is a genuine joy to behold. As each one narrates his week's history, he scowls or chortles just as if he were reliving the moment all over again. And the others laugh with him and join the story telling, and all within a few feet of where they will hear in a few minutes the greatest story of all repeated again.

In a real sense Sunday morning is the one time in the week when your story and your people's story and God's story all intersect. The story line which has opened onto a hundred sidepaths during the week suddenly converges again and reminds us that as diverse as our lives may be, we are all seeking the same conclusion; we are all wanting the eternal Author to bring us in the end to the beginning, to the fragrant Paradise of God.

As pastor, when you sit on the podium on Sunday morning, your eyes panning your people, a number of thoughts rather foreign to the sermon usually cross your mind. As your eyes range across the congregation, a few of the people rivet your attention more than others.

You usually see the treasurer. Even if you didn't know him at all, you could tell by watching him over the course of a Sunday morning that he has a sense of the importance of his task. If churches were businesses, most of them would be hopelessly doomed to bankruptcy. Sunday after Sunday the treasurer holds his breath as he hits the total button on the calculator. Will there be enough dollars to pay the pastor and fend off the creditors and send the missionaries? Will there be any left over to repair the leaky roof? On the first Sunday of the month, he isn't quite as panicky, but by the fourth or fifth Sunday, the treasurer lives in a cold sweat, ready to pinch every piece of copper he can find. If treasurers ever dread to go to church, their fifth Sundays must be unbearable. Because no matter what you say, the treasurer is right: a church lives on the brink.

There are probably a great many gray-haired treasurers who worried their way to that color, but the fact remains that churches continue on when by all practical standards they should have been dead by debt. It's pretty hard to convince your treasurer of that, but it's true nonetheless.

And there's a reason for it. Churches have one thing going for them that doesn't characterize any other enterprise—the miracle of generosity. When crunch time comes, the word *sacrifice* begins to crop up, and the people who were already giving cheerfully shell out even more. When Eastern Airlines tested the generosity of its people, it ended up filing for Chapter 11. But again and again a little group of people not even large enough to fill up a single plane have responded to God and at his urging caused a miracle of money. The church has been spared default and embarrassment, and on the following Sunday you would hardly know that the beautiful people who sit quietly in the pews have given way out of proportion to anything you will ever see in the secular world.

Then there's another man in the congregation who usually gets your attention because of the obvious incongruity. He has just hit the mysterious age of forty. I don't know what it is, but there seems to be a disease that strikes forty-year-old men that makes them want to act as if they are twenty. And he's got it. He has begun to unbutton his shirt collar so his chest hair will show, and recently he bought a gold pendant with a pocket watch for the emblem, and when he walks he reminds you of Big Ben on a stroll. His wife is a little worried. She's afraid that he's eyeing a younger girl. She may be right. But have you ever wondered why a man that age would chase a twenty-year-old? It must be a lot like a dog chasing a car. After he catches her, what's he going to do about it? Frankly I hope I can help him before his feelings go too far.

There's a young couple over there whose children are already (at ages three and five) wearing the pants in the family. They talk right out in church and look at their parents as if to say, "So, what are you gonna' do about it?" And they talk out at the wrong times. While we're in the middle of the Apostles' Creed, about ready to descend into hell, they are worried about making it to the bathroom. It's a perennial delight to watch older couples sitting around them trying to manage their anger. Their children of course never breathed in church and here sit these urchins, breathing and blathering and sneering to boot. I'd give five dollars to have a picture of one grandfather's face when he turns and tries to stare down those children. He probably would prefer to keep to the King James Version's, "Suffer the little children to come unto me." To be honest, I would hate for that family to move. Sunday mornings wouldn't be quite the same without them.

But everybody usually survives the antics, and I remember again that Sundays are as much for children as they are for adults and in spite of the commotion, we all come together and even if only in intervals, God's Word gets through.

Then there's one dear lady in our church who sits in the same pew and sings the same note every week no matter what page all the rest of the people are on. When she stands to testify, you can almost feel the whole crowd groan. She has several good statements to make, but she has no idea when she's finished. I feel about her like William Jennings Bryan's mother felt about him. One day after he had given a two-hour oration, he sat down beside her to receive her praise, "Well, Billy," she said, "you missed two good opportunities to sit down!" Elsie is that way. She will say several helpful things, but that is largely because she says so much that she could hardly miss altogether. By the time she's back down in her pew, we know how much water it takes to sprinkle her garden and where she dropped her keys on the way to the grocery store. Every church needs at least one "Elsie" but there also should be a quota!

We enjoy talking about Jesus and the twelve disciples he chose and how different they were. But most of us have an equally amazing assortment of people who fill our pews and seek God's way. As one pastor phrased it, we also have our "uncommon people who have an extraordinary capacity for performing uncommon labors of love."

Sunday mornings have a way of blending people into a unity that can only be described as divine. When we sit on the platform and feel the joy of belonging as it surges in our soul, we do well to remind ourselves again that really, all we are doing is standing at a different tabernacle and motioning to our people and pointing to the cloud. One pastor expressed it like this, "If I could explain everything about my church, chances are, God wouldn't be in it." It is a mystery. Your people know that they could speak with God at home. But they also know that there's glory in the tabernacle. So they come together. For one grand moment they come from their tents and turn their eyes upon Jesus. It is a long journey, this journey through the wilderness, and they, like you, know they will travel it best if they come together and get their bearings from God.

5

Called a Friend of God

Celebrating Your Likeness to God

The people who eventually make it into the history books are usually remembered for one great feat or characteristic. Out of the long list of activities, one event usually rises above the rest as the clue by which the rest of that person's life is remembered. Jonah had a whale of a time, Samson flexed his muscles, and Hosea married a wife.

In the case of Noah things are different. Though the Bible does not devote page after page to his life, it says enough in a few short strokes to let him be remembered for any one of a number of things. Looking back we might say he belongs in the memory because he saw the first rain and rainbow, or because he built the first floating zoo, or because his life of faith made possible the rest of civilization. As pastors we might remember him as the man who preached for more than a century without a single convert outside his own family!

If Noah were writing his autobiography, the highlights listed above would probably get no better than honorable mention. For him the first place prize in life's achievement awards would be his ranking as a friend of God. Long

73

before the ark and the flood and the olive branch are ever mentioned, there is another phrase in Genesis 6 which Noah would have placed in the center of all reflection on his life. Among the cluster of descriptive phrases that surround his life this one stands at the summit: Noah walked with God. The rainbow was pretty and the ark was useful, but they were at best passing claims to fame. Long after the rainbow had vanished in the morning sun and the ark rotted on Mount Ararat, Noah's yearning to be like God was only just begun.

If he could have picked the accomplishment for which he would be most remembered, he would have gone with that which mattered most in the shaping of his soul—his permanent relationship with God. What he would have celebrated most would have been the fact that in this matter of choosing friends after whom to model his life, he had hit on the very best. His model was God. When the door finally closed on his earthly life, he knew that he had made his share of mistakes and he regretted that. But in all his living, he had tried more than anything else to live as much as possible like God.

Any pastor who looks back across the path of his ministry sees what Noah saw. Victories and defeats lay scattered all about. As you look back, you can point out people who came to know Christ because you cared. You can tell of a marriage that held together because you offered repair. You can tell of a stubborn husband who never did respond to your offer of help. You could speak with pride about buildings and dollars and attendance figures. You could talk about Sundays when the offering would hardly buy a bus ticket out of town. But when you sit down to sort out what matters most about your work, you will always revel most in the fact that your ministry sprang out of a desire to follow in the footsteps of Jesus.

Not everything you touch turns to gold, but you celebrate the fact that more things are lovely in your ministry than would have been if you hadn't come along. The purity in your heart may not always have made it into practice, but at least you know it was there, and it tempered all your work with the soft glow of God.

No matter how hard we try, we will never be in the same orbit with God. He alone will occupy the category that we call divine. As pastors we can never advertise as his equal although a few seem bent on trying. What we ought to celebrate rather is our resemblance to him, our likeness to his image. We take pride in the point that what turns his head turns ours. What gnaws at his sense of holiness eats away at ours as well. What thrills him thrills us. He is the supreme overshepherd, and we are only local shepherds, but like him we have a heart for the sheep. We may be distinguished from him in the size of our sheepcote and the dimensions of our love, but when we pull back the cover from our heart, we discover that it is beating in rhythm with his. Just as a duplicate is never quite like the original, so we will never look exactly like God. But we must remind ourselves that even if our image of him is blurry and dull, at least like Mary of New Testament fame, we have chosen the good part, and it shall not be taken away from us. At least we have aimed as high as the human soul can ever go. And the very aspiration can only enable our soul.

So we stand with our people at the edge of eternity and point them in the direction where God lives. We know that we are not God, nor even in the same league with him, but we take seriously our call to live as close to him as we can so that we can keep getting a clear picture of how he looks and what he likes. We want to be sure as we point people in his direction that we are close enough ourselves to make our directions worth following. Only as we stay within earshot of him will we be able to tell others clearly what we have seen and heard. At times we may despair of even doing that. There are days when we feel so down that we are sure that we are a definite liability to the kingdom, let alone a model worth following.

The fact that a pastor is above all else a friend of God

hints of one of the most fascinating facts about a very public man—he is also a very private soul. Like the God whom
he seeks to imitate, there are some facts about him that his
people will never know. A few things in his mind will
always remain there for only him and God to share.

Frankly there are a number of thoughts that pass
through your mind as a pastor that your people should
never know. Even though you are the spiritual leader and
probably as mature as most of your people, you still feel
most of the feelings that other people feel. If all your inner
ecstacies and agonies got flashed on a public screen, you
would be embarrassed, and your board would probably
have your eviction notice in the mail. When it gets right
down to it, a few of the people in your church are duds as
leaders and not much better suited as followers. Most of
them give you cause to hope, but a handful make you
wonder at times if God didn't create a few people in order
for heaven to have its humor. You have your personal
opinions about your people that you have to keep under
lock and key. You might wish you didn't have to know so
much about a few people and could forget what you know
about others. Your knowledge can so easily color your
behavior and give you away at times. But you keep striv-
ing to strike a public balance because showing favorites is
not fitting to a follower of God.

This doesn't mean that a pastor is dishonest if he shields
his people from his personal views. It simply means that
he as leader knows that he must live by the biblical rule of
impartiality and not by whim of personal preference.
Every Christian should do that. The pastor must do it to an
extreme.

There are several other facts that the people in the pew
rarely know about you. A few of the more perceptive
might catch it, but for the most part your people would
never know it when you fall into a spiritual slump. They
may chide you for not feeding them well from the pulpit
or for being a jot dry, but they would rarely be able to pinpoint the time when you bottomed out in your own soul.

Unless you tell them, it is also true that they would have no idea how often you feel inadequate to your task. The wise pastor will reveal himself partially because he belongs in the human category and wants his people to know it clearly. However, he must never reveal himself fully, or else he will lose much of the respect he has earned through the years. That's a tough balance to strike, but the public and private side of the pastor need to be held in tension, or else the private man becomes an embarrassing exhibitionist. Like God, the pastor must never divulge all his secrets or he will no longer be a listening shepherd in whom to confide but a public tattletale deserving our sneers.

Try as hard as they might, it is hard for a group of people to let their pastor be as human as they are. They want a moral model and a spiritual giant. While every pastor worries that he is neither, he is nevertheless pulled up higher by the fact that he dares not disappoint his people. He may not be completely comfortable with the perception that he is living at a higher moral level, but he celebrates his growth which comes about by the stimulus of expectation and moves ahead.

The little girl holding the sketch pencil in hand was probably more confident than a pastor should ever be, but she spoke in the right direction. When her mother asked her what she was drawing she replied, "A picture of God." "Why, honey," her mother reprimanded, "you can't draw God. Nobody knows what he looks like." The little girl shot back, "They will when I get finished."

On the inside the pastor rarely feels that sure of his showing. If the people who watch him get only a strong hint of what God is like he will be satisfied.

For all his public profile, most of what a pastor does is first brought to life in the quiet ways of his mind. As he and God dialogue and think together, they set in motion the basic beliefs that will eventually work their way into his public performance. Therefore, as a pastor, you should not only celebrate your private time with God but also guard it carefully. Out of it grows the public man. If elevating thoughts about your people form the atmosphere of your mind, then a noble relationship can develop with most if not all of your people. A few people (often powerful ones) can bend and even break your hope—even in its strongest moments—but on average, if you refuse to give up on a friendship, no matter how strained, you are often rewarded with restoration in the end. The better your set of assumptions about your people the better will be your behavior before them. The higher you hold your soul toward God, the closer your people will be able to draw as well. For all of its apparent publicity, a magnificent ministry is, at its beginning, a silent seedling in the soul. When you revel in an outward accomplishment, you need to trace it back to its roots. If you stay with it long enough, you will probably find that it got started one night as you sat by the fireplace wondering how you could be a better pastor to the people in your fold, or as you reflected on how you could model the Master better to the masses.

As pastors we will never circle in the same level with God but we can move in the same sphere and in the same direction. The level of his love will always surpass our own, but his global love does not cancel the need for our more local type. In fact one of the best expressions of his universal love is through our around-town living. It will not be nearly as influential as God's because we are bound to a specific time and space, but it can be similar in quality.

In a CBS special Bill Moyers was reporting on a man in New York City who made it a point every day on his way to work to hand out a hundred sandwiches. Street people learned about his love and lined the sidewalks to get a bite of food. After showing a clip of the man in action handing out his sandwiches, Moyers said, "New York City's population now runs in excess of eleven million people. A hundred sandwiches will hardly scratch the surface of the need. But while Sam may never move his world very far, at least the direction he is moving it is forward." That's what pastors do too. And they do it for the most part because they are trying to model after God.

When you take time to reflect on what really motivates you most in your ministry, several assumptions will come into focus. Each one is a special point of praise all by itself. But when taken together, they form a core of convictions that confirms to you again and again that you walk best before your people when you stay near to the heart of God. Friendship with him means insight for them.

Since the pastor's public life is little more than the cover pulled away from his private thoughts, he deserves to celebrate the nearness of his own mind to the mind of God. Whatever genuine success he has in pastoring will hinge on how well he imitates the Savior in thought, word, and deed. Any pastor who has had even the tiniest touch of success in his work has at some point along the way copied the Christ who pioneered the plan of seeking and saving the lost. If he has had good results in his work, he must credit the Lord for making him a decent copy of himself.

Several great similarities between the pastor and God belong in our daily memory. It is part of the majesty of ministry that the pastor above all else is modeling for God. For most of the people in the congregation, his thoughts reflect God's thoughts and his heart God's heart.

Like God, you as pastor can revel in the thought that you continue to believe in your people in spite of all you know about them. As pastor you learn over time to see people clearly without feeling that their foibles and failures deprive them of beauty. You learn to love each one as a unique human spirit, unparalleled in its stark beauty. Sure, you will meet your quota of people whose personalities contain a natural repellent. But God compensates for that by giving you a dozen others who can do no wrong. And you keep believing in them both.

Believing in people means trusting them to make choices for themselves. As the Good Shepherd, God did that too. He ran the risk of free will. And he lost. But the

whole tone of the Bible is biased with the belief that God
still believes in us and wants to trust us with his work.

In working with people, you win by believing that every
person you meet is a treasury of free ideas. Every person
you meet knows more about something than you do. They
have personal agendas which need to be recognized and
woven in. When you go into a meeting you may have three
or four ideas you would love to see adopted. But you will
leave happier if you start by saying to yourself, "Hey, I
have these ideas, but if I don't get every item I ask for, I
still want to be happy because I am a team player and
these people have excellent thoughts as well."

Infallibility is an attitude. It creeps into the spirit and
hinders us from hearing and helping others. Barriers rise
quickly when people bring rigid agendas into group ses-
sions. As a pastor you lose only if you meet rigidity with
rigidity. So you have an unbudging board member. You
win over that attitude, not by stern resistance, but by
allowing that member's ideas to be aired and then letting
the vote be the law. If the board votes with the unyielding
member, so be it. You may need to think of moving. But
you never win when you flair up in force to quash your
opponents.

There's no easy way to deal with rigid resistance in
groups. A man convinced against his will is of the same
opinion still. Occasionally you have to give up your run at
infallibility and go with the flow. The tendency is to
squelch people or at least want to. But experience tells us
that it's a losing strategy.

One simple but successful strategy for dealing with people in a group setting is to deal with the members' personal agendas before you work with the official agenda.
Take time to ask them personally how the week has gone
and how their families are going and then the official matters will be opened in a context of bonding and warmth. It
may take fifteen minutes to open the personal worlds of
the members, but that fifteen minutes will make the other
forty-five flow more smoothly than a full hour without it.

Try It

In your local board meetings you might want to change your approach to include a longer time for personal interchange with your board members. Before launching into the items on the agenda, engage them in body life, board-meeting style. Take ten or fifteen minutes or more to bring everybody up to date and to pray for any needs represented by the group.

You must remember that just because people know each other does not automatically mean that they instantly relate. The beginning of any board meeting has a time of detachment and coolness among the members. That's not because they aren't friendly. It happens because they are coming suddenly from totally different settings with no common points of contact for the past few hours. If you will take the time to unify their minds around shared personal experiences and agendas, you will have better success in uniting them about the church's needs.

The pastor should celebrate the daily joy of joining with God in shaping the minds of his people. Ministry that truly matures people is a matter of years, never of the moments. Any group of people bent on a common destiny needs a leader who keeps on pointing them clearly and persistently toward God. The shaping of the soul is rarely the stroke of an instant. It may take only a moment to save the soul, but it takes a lifetime to change the mind. Only by a steady biblical diet week after week can the transformation finally occur. At times the congregation may feel that it would like to hold onto an evangelist or a concert artist who happens by. His charisma or personal appeal may inspire a few to think that he would be a better leader than the pastor, but that feeling is usually superficial. In instances where the evangelist has been called back to assume the pastorate, churches discover that their eyes were bigger than their stomach, that he didn't have the qualities which fitted him for devoted daily pastoral care after all.

As a visiting preacher to one congregation, I remember the note written to me by the pastor's daughter. Her spelling may have been elementary, but her sentiment was mature: "I thank you are the best precher, eccept my dad and grandpa. P.S. An a few others."

As a pastor we should expect that many of our people on the spur of the moment will chase off after every hit-and-run preacher who passes through the neighborhood, but we should never mistake their sudden enthrallment with another for their lasting preference for us. If we do, we are threatened by outsiders and cannot fully appreciate the fresh ideas and perspective they bring to our people. We do well to smile at the infatuation of the moment and remind ourselves that we too enjoyed about seven days of halo and honeymoon.

What we as pastors offer our people is the gift of continuity. For any permanent spiritual maturity to occur, there must be a consistent discipleship. That can only occur when one leader is allowed to spend an extended period of time with the people whom he is developing.

Often you meet people in churches who pride themselves on having sat in every seminar on spiritual formation that has been held within a hundred miles. I'm usually not impressed. People who run off to every big-name speaker who comes by are frequently as haphazard and undisciplined in their spiritual lives as they are in their scavenging for seminars. The steady discipline of submitting to the ministry of one pastor is in itself one of the indicators of spiritual maturity. People who refuse to submit to a single spiritual leader for most of their spiritual growth are not to be praised but pitied. To lurch from leader to leader only locks the soul in a pattern of restlessness that eventually threatens even the most stable of spiritual commitments. It trains the heart to always be looking for some new fad or fancy because it *is* new and not because it is helpful. When that occurs, religion can so easily become a search for the latest trend instead of dedication to a healthy habit.

Another area in which the pastor can celebrate his like-ness to God is in this matter of personal integrity. As he lives in close harmony with God, the pastor more and more reflects the holy character of his model. Of all the things that we as pastors do, being a friend of God is the one fact that can never be unraveled by outside events. Buildings can burn down, renewals turn sour, and the whole church collapse in a heap of bitterness and shame. But our relationship with God is so incredibly inward that it cannot be destroyed by any outward event no matter how terrible or tiny. Our friendship with God is the one untouchable constant of our personal faith. Everything in our ministry may be taken away from us, but we can still celebrate the salvation of our soul. One pastor who ran head-on into a financial cul-de-sac that threatened to shut down his ministry said that one day as he was praying and wrestling with the terrible sins of failure in his financial management, he was overwhelmed in his heart by a sud-den rush of these simple words, "Jesus loves me, this I know, for the Bible tells me so." "For several days," he said, "I went in the strength of that simple line. I was God's. And if I had failed, at least I had failed for the right Person, and for the right reasons."

A generation ago the sin which got its fair share and more of preaching time was that of pride. In recent years there has been a trend in pulpits as well as in society to shift away from pride to integrity. Greater scrutiny of the private lives of public figures will be remembered as a prominent feature of our times. For the pastor that trend cuts two ways. It demands that he give more attention than ever to keeping his house in order. The fishbowl is not only being looked at, it is being entered and searched. The slipup of a few has led to the scrutiny of the many. Our integrity may not be less thorough than it ever was, but we may be sure that it will no longer go unexamined. People are concerned more and more that the people who lead them be as holy in their private lives as they claim in their public sermons.

For the man of purity this closer attention brings a surprise opportunity. It gives him a chance to model what he preaches and have it seriously looked at. If the two messages coincide—the spoken and the living—the pastor gets two messages for the price of one. If people choose to look at our lives, why not take advantage of it and let their look convince them that what we say is what in fact we do. If they can see that what we say is being lived out in us, our second sermon will only echo our first—the one in life. We have long praised the "sermon in shoes" as the strongest one we have. If society is backing up that view, then we as pastors are standing at the edge of an enormous opportunity. For the first time in a long time people are looking at the larger scope of our lives. That means more influence. More of what we say and do counts. Our time away from the church is beginning to figure alongside our time at the church. If we live well, we speak right twice. As communicators of the gospel we welcome and celebrate that.

As a pastor you can also rejoice in your likeness to God when you face the pain of persecution. Sometimes the sheep smite the shepherd. Unless you are highly unusual, you will face a major round of resistance at some point along the way of your ministry. Even the most successful of pastors face it. Even God continues to face it. Because of his size, God can deal with it without having to regroup and look elsewhere as we often do. But make no mistake, Calvary was not the end of God's troubles.

As much as we would like for it to be different, there are times when persecution pressures push us to rethink our ministry setting. There are several criteria a pastor ought to consider when he sits down to decide whether to stay at a particular church or make a move. Here are a few indicators worth watching when you are dealing with the question of how to know when to go. No single one of these criteria for leaving a church is reason by itself to cause us to go somewhere else. But as a group, these factors should lead us to give serious attention to a new area of service and ministry before we crash in a heap and forsake God's call altogether.

As you mull over the issue of whether to stay or go, consider these questions:

1. *Do you struggle with a persistent inability to feel any inspiration for your preaching?* A sustained struggle to experience God's anointing either in the study or in the pulpit is cause for concern.

2. *Do you feel a steady resistance from the people to several of your goals for the church which you feel you simply cannot compromise?* If there is no hope for your deepest desires for that ministry to ever move beyond the paper on which they are written, you may need to explore the possibility of finding a new setting in which the people are open to your vision.

3. *Are you getting mixed signals from the people whom you consider your most loyal supporters?* Take this example of a mixed signal, "Pastor, you know how much we appreciate your ministry, but because of the pressures on you and your family, we wonder if it wouldn't be better if we voted for a change?" That kind of statement is an early-warning device worth hearing and considering.

4. *Is your family under undue stress because of their involvement with you as a member of the pastoral family?* When pressures from the church invade the parsonage to the point of family tension and potential breakdown, the time for change is close at hand.

5. *Do you find that your defensive responses are beginning to outnumber your offensive ones.* As George Will once said, "When you're defending, you're losing."

6. *Will you receive a substantial block of negative votes from people in your church whose vote counts for more than one?* Not every person in the church counts for the same when it comes to a pastoral vote. As a pastor you know fairly quickly who counts more than one. If the number of influential persons who would vote against you is high, you have all the more reason to consider a change. Most of the time, we can know

well in advance the way the vote will swing. If you act carefully, yet promptly, you may be able to save you and your family the pain and the church the embarrassment.

Abraham Lincoln was right. You do destroy an enemy when you make him your friend. It is also true that not every person is willing to leave his/her enemy status. A few will always prefer to live in that mind-set. And when they do, the wise pastor recognizes that fact and like God accepts the hard reality that for some people he will never be fully welcomed.

The hockey goalie raised a good question. "How would you like it," he said, "if every time you made a mistake, a horn blared, a red light flashed on and fifteen thousand people booed?"

For most pastors thankfully it's not that dramatic, but it sure can seem awfully close. As the bridge between God and people and also people and people, you are bound to get walked on. And it's far easier to say than to believe, but there is probably no point at which we can more fully identify with God than in filling up the sufferings of Christ. At times the unfairness of your people is little more than irksome. You and your wife are invited to a banquet and the host forgets to pay for her meal. So you dip into your meager honorarium to cover for her and wind up barely breaking even. Or you perform a Saturday wedding for free only to have to stay late into the night cleaning up the flower petals and mud that the love-dazed couple left behind.

At other times the scene convulses with hate. One pastor told of having his answering machine splattered with four letter words and terms such as *scum, nerd* and *bastard*. I understood when he told of the anger that blew sky high in his heart. A minister without such a horror story is probably either very young or very fortunate. Ministry is often messy and sloppy with enough people slashing and blustering their way around to stamp out the vision of the average person. But still we care, or at least try to, and go on with God. The scars from such encounters are often glaring and last for a long time. As we walk away from the scene of the crime that has been perpetrated against us, we need to remember that God once did that too.

In his likeness to God the pastor can also celebrate his steady burden for his people. There never is a time day or night when he can chuck his responsibility for a fling of uncaring freedom. No matter how far he may travel, even on vacation, he remembers that part of his heart belongs at home, home with his people whom God has put under his twenty-four-hour care.

God doesn't toss his burdens around lightly. He entrusts them to people who will tend them well and carry them seriously. At a golf course in Gatlinburg, Tennessee, I asked the man behind the desk about their group rates. His answer took me by surprise, "I don't know anything about that," he said. "I just work here."

The pastor who lives to love people never lays down his burden. He is responsible. That is both a heavy weight and a tremendous wonder. The care of the congregation belongs to him. He may enjoy parts of his work more than others, but the whole work is his, and his great call is to love people. He may enjoy the details of building a new sanctuary or the thrill of setting new goals, but the people who will help to live out his dreams are his chief care.

Try It

You've occasionally heard someone quip, "Well, a pastor doesn't do too bad on salary when you consider that he only works about an hour or two a week. A few words on Sunday and that's about it. That must be fun."

But you could hardly find a vocation that ranks with pastoring for the subtle factors of the job that never make the job description. Think about it for a moment. What do you do in the course of a week that even your most dedicated people would not think about as draining your heart and your time? Take this for a starting list:

1. The twenty-four-hour responsibility from which you cannot be free, even on vacations. You always need to leave behind a number to call in case of emergency.
2. The radical changes you often have to make in your schedule in order to cope with a crisis.
3. The decision-making energy you expend on such items as what you will preach on next Sunday, what people should you visit this week, or when will you start on that capital campaign?
4. The constant balancing act between family and church. Are you spending enough time with the people and too little with your family or vice versa? Can you even strike a balance, or is it a matter that you need to be always evaluating?

A bus driver in the western suburbs of Chicago made the point. One day he came barreling along his route only to bypass people at several of his stops. There they stood on the curb, flailing their arms to get his attention, but he zoomed on by, waving as he went. By the time he got to the station the manager's phone was ringing off the wall.

"Hey, Jack!" the manager was furious. "What in the world do you mean? Didn't you see all those people standing at the stops wanting to ride? What in the dickens were you doing?"

"Well," said Jack, "I had to make a decision. I had to decide whether to be on time or haul people, and today I decided to be on time!"

I don't know what happened to Jack and his future with the bus company, but for the pastor there really is no option. We will always err on the side of hauling people. We will always have goals and plans that reach far into the future. We will often have to live for a time in the dogged pursuit of the clock. But the clock and the calendar must never be allowed to dictate our work at the expense of our primary concern—the care of our people.

In pastoral ministry you will always want to get there, but you will also want to be sure and make all the stops along the way. Far from being driven by programs and torn by timetables, the pastor will want to sit down with his people and help them by holding their hurts in his heart. He will so care for his people that they will have the attitude of one mother toward her pediatrician, "Dr. Jesch makes you feel that she got her MD just to care for your child." That may mean months and even years when there is no outward sign of progress. But it is foolish to gloss over pain in order to meet a goal. Helping people always comes first. And sometimes it takes a long time to bring people to a point where they are genuinely able to go forward. The healing of damaged emotions may not make headlines, but it is necessary before we get too carried away with other people's views of success.

No pastor worth his salt ever assumes that he has finally arrived in his work, that he is now doing it exactly like God himself would do. While he is pointing his people upward, he knows all too well that he himself is still searching for ways to be more like God. The search is unending, the desire unquenched.

It is also a joy to know that we are aiming nobly, that our hearts are set on becoming as close an imitator of the Master as we possibly can. And we will do that best if we keep on tagging along behind him as he travels his high and holy way.

Ray pastors a church in Indiana. One day as he was leaving for his office across the street, his five-year-old son, Ray, Jr., came running up behind him.

"Daddy," he said, "Can I go with you to the office for a while?"

Ray thought it was a good idea so he called back to inform his wife, Sue, and across the street they went.

Once in the office, Ray sat down and began sorting through his workload for the morning while Ray, Jr., stood silently in the door. For several minutes Ray kept to his work, not noticing his son by the door nor the seriousness on the five-year-old's face. Finally he turned toward him. The silence had gotten his attention. "Son, are you okay? I

haven't heard you. You must have been standing pretty
still."

"Yeah, Dad, I'm okay."

A few more moments passed and still the little boy
didn't move. He kept looking at his father and the desk
full of work. Ray turned to him again.

"Son, are you sure you're okay? You're being awfully
quiet."

"Yeah, I'm okay. Hey, Dad," the tone had changed.
"Dad, where do you keep your sermons?"

Ray laughed. "Right over here in this filing cabinet.
Why? What are you thinking?"

"Well, Dad," said the little boy, "I was thinking, if someday something happens to you and you get sick and can't
preach, I need to know where they are so I can be ready!"

Ray said the statement floored him and thrilled him all
at the same time. "More than ever before," he said, "I knew
how much my son was wanting to walk in my shoes. That
day I vowed to be a better man so that I wouldn't have a
problem if my son decided to use my shoes and walk my
way."

As pastors we will never be the Senior Shepherd. At best
we will be the "little Rays." We will watch God and want
to grow up to be just like him.

There is hardly anything that we could give our people
that would be of more benefit to them than our friendship
with God. If they can know that we are reflecting the
Father's will to the best of our abilities, they will also know
that they are becoming more like him themselves. We may
never save a whole civilization as Noah did, but as we continue to mold our minds in the shape of the Master's, we
too can be assured that for our time and place we too are
helping to construct an ark to the saving of our house.

6

A Still, Small Voice

Celebrating God's Unique Visitations

If you were charting Elijah's moods on a graph, when you came to 1 Kings 19 the pen would be down at the bottom of the page. Just hours after scoring the biggest knock-out of his career against 850 prophets of Baal, he is lying under a juniper tree begging to die. His shocking walk-away had hardly made it to press when he finds himself in the darkest night of his soul. He had prayed a short prayer, and God had opened the sky and rained out enough fire to scorch even the sweltering desert sand. No doubt about it, Mount Carmel was the stroke of a lifetime. If any story would make the news, that one would. It had all the stuff of stories: Ahab and Jezebel steamed, a valley full of corpses, a local cloudburst to wash up the mess, a head-and-shoulders hero. Enough to make movie producers salivate.

There was just one catch. Elijah didn't stick around to see the show. The rumor spread around that the King and Queen had more than a passing interest in seeing Elijah join the victims in the valley, and Elijah was off and running for his life. Just to make sure he got safely out of firing range, he went as far south in Judah as he could go, and then just to make real sure, he went one more day's trek into the desert. Before he dropped in the sand under the tree, he probably glanced over his shoulder one more time just in case. In more ways than one, Elijah was bushed!

Then God did something that Elijah probably experienced only once in his lifetime—God fixed his food. Elijah ate and slept and ate and slept. It was the kind of divine R and R which pastors would give up a holiday Sunday just to enjoy. It should have been enough to help Elijah shake his mood, and move out of the doldrums, but it didn't. He headed off to Mount Horeb with his heart still behind him under the juniper tree. All along the way he whined about his solitary confinement as a God-fearing man. He complained about the people whom he was supposed to be helping. Elijah was in a bad way. And God knew it. And God also knew just what to do.

One morning as Elijah was about to drop the needle on the same old broken record, "*I only . . . I only. . . .*" God got to the point.

"Elijah!"

"Yes, God."

"Elijah, go over there and climb that mountain. I want to show you something."

Elijah climbed. "Okay, God, I'm ready. What is it?"

No sooner had he spoken than a tornado ripped down the mountain knocking over boulders and splintering trees on the way. When the debris and dust had settled a little, Elijah cupped his ear and waited for God to explain it all—but nothing came. Not a sound. Silence. Seconds later a fault line ripped along the side of the mountain scattering rocks like marbles, leveling the ridges, and gaping the ground beneath his feet. Elijah was all ears now. Surely God was about to talk. Again Elijah waited for the interpretation—but nothing came.

Then a bolt of lightning seared the ground at his feet and Elijah thought, *Okay, God, either you're being redundant or I'm being dull. What are you trying to say?* But as hard as he listened—not a sound. Breathless quiet.

Then he heard it. In the lull while he was waiting for another pounding boom or bang to shake the mountain in another way, it came. At first it sounded like a low whisper, like a person exhaling a gentle lung-cleansing breath. In the Hebrew language the term used is our expression for a sigh. He held his breath so he could listen more closely. And sure enough. It was something more than a breeze blowing. It was more distinct than the ripple of a brook, more precise than the wind in the leaves. He had never heard it quite that way before, but he had heard it enough to know in his inner soul that he was once again at the edge of a great mystery. Once again he was hearing the vivid voice of God. The tender tramp of divine feet was once again marching in his soul.

As he stood, not daring to move for fear of losing the voice in the shuffle, he reached for his mantle. He had held it many times as a symbol of God's power at work in his life. This time he held it even over his face as a symbol of his awareness that he was near to the heart of God. This was the true knowledge of the holy. If he were reading all the signals clearly, God was about to pay him the visit of a lifetime, and he wanted to make sure that he had done all he could do to prepare the way of the Lord.

As he stood in the door of the cave, his mantle shielding his face from the blazing holiness of God, Elijah knew again the breathtaking beauty of beholding God.

I doubt he ever forgot that cave. As the years went along, if he ever passed by that way again, he must have pointed over to the very spot where he was standing when, instead of finding God in the loud rumbling of a storm, he found him in the quiet pulsations of his soul. On his down days he must have remembered the juniper tree, but on his God-filled days he must have remembered the cave.

Every worship season is beautiful, but on rare occasions the Spirit moves in so near that the scene is dazzling with a sacred shimmer. You can never finally predict how he will come, by what door, or through which person, but once in a while, God pulls out all the stops. A worship service that was elevating suddenly becomes heavenly. It shifts to a higher plain of power. An energy superior to human emotion and more powerful than the combined forces of earth flows through every person in the sanctuary, saint and sinner alike. People who thought they would remain tough turn tender. People who didn't know they could even speak about God in public become frankly garrulous. Like a tidal wave billowing through the pews, the Spirit streams into the hearts of the hearers and assumes control of the worship flow. To be God's person, called to give whatever human leadership may be needed in a service like that is one of the highest honors a human being will ever know. For a while, the gap which you had been trying to bridge between your people and God is bridged by God himself.

There are several features of a unique visit from God that always surprise the mind and thrill the heart at their coming. There are several fascinating happenings when God stops by in person. For one, you will never find a calendar of the church year anywhere that can pinpoint when it will happen. Part of the marvel of such a moment, in fact, is the insight that God alone had it on his schedule and knew just when to set it in motion. We should never chuck the bulletin in order to try to force God's hand, in order to try to *make* him make something happen. But neither must the bulletin become a barrier. If God reaches down and asks to rewrite the order of worship on special occasions, we should hand it over promptly because he clearly has something in mind.

A pastor in a southern state described how a special surge from the Spirit swept through his church one Sunday morning. To his knowledge nothing unusual had happened that week to hint of the event. In fact, the previous week's service, though uplifting, showed no sign that its successor would be unforgettable. At the outset that service too was moving according to plan. The hymn they had sung to open the Sunday school "Blessed Redeemer," they had sung a hundred times. Hardly anyone needed a hymnal for it anymore. The Sunday school superintendent was hardly an orator even on his better occasions and that morning was not one of his better occasions. He mumbled through a few opening comments about like usual. Then he prayed his regular prayer and dismissed the people to Sunday school—all in one breath. But nobody got up to go. Thinking that he had not communicated clearly, he started back at the prayer and did the last part over again. Only this time when he gave the dismissal, he made a large flourish with his hands. They certainly couldn't miss that. But still nobody moved.

A little confused, but at the edge of a deep perception, the superintendent walked back to his seat on the platform. No sooner had he sat down than a red-haired man whose heart had recently been shredded by a divorce stood and raised his hand.

"I just wanted to thank God for how good he's been to me," he said, and sat down.

The pastor later said, "When that man testified, it was like opening a bottle of fragrance from heaven. The Spirit spread around like divine perfume. For two hours the people testified and prayed and sang and wept. Over one hundred people voluntarily visited the altar. It was a day that will live forever in my heart and in my memory."

But true to form, every silver lining also has a cloud. At the end of the service, the Sunday school secretary, who had missed most of the power because she was in the basement counting pennies, came running up the stairs frustrated.

"Pastor, pastor, I don't know what to do about the attendance. Pastor, nobody went to class. I don't think anybody got counted. What are we going to do, Pastor? What about the numbers on the board?"

Said the pastor, "The sad scene of a little mind at such a grand occasion broke my heart."

"Forget the numbers," he told her. "Today was more

than numbers. Just cut a piece of cardboard and slip it in the slot on the board and write on it, ' God came.'"

If we knew God's timing on everything, he would no longer be God. If all his plans were in our datebook, we would have him flattened down to human height, and for him that's way too low. The mystery of his ministry is part of its marvel. Jesus put it well, "It is not for you to know the times or dates the Father has set by his own authority" (Acts 1:7). When one-of-a-kind services occur, we are only enjoying a gentle reminder that God's ways are still higher than our ways and his thoughts exceed our own.

It is a high moment of celebration for the pastor when the Holy Spirit visits the worship with more obviousness than at other times. It is always true that where two or three gather in Christ's name, he is there, but sometimes he is so there that his presence dominates everything, even the structure of the service. Suddenly, gently, the flow of worship is lifted to a higher plain. A mood of restrained expectancy hovers above the people. Minds that had been wandering out to the golf course or over to the market scurry back to see what will happen next. All across the congregation a spirit of solemn unity grips the people. Often the most reverent gift of the moment is silence.

God's power-packed visits are also quite rare. For most of us, the event is so uncommon that we could probably count on our two hands the times we've seen it. But for all its rarity, when it does occur, a pastor can go on the strength of the memory for many days.

It is probably by design that God keeps such moments rare. If we enjoyed them too often, their very commonness would diminish their startling beauty. Moses only had one burning bush. Peter walked on the water only once. Ezekiel witnessed only one wheel. The very fact that such moments remain unpredictable and rare helps them retain their mystery and majesty which are so fitting to God. Perhaps in heaven, monotony from repetition will be suspended, but for now the very scarceness of God's vivid nearness makes it all the more wonderful in its coming.

While God always wants to figure in our daily round, he also wants to remain the transcendent one. He wants us to remember that eternity alone is a large enough house for One who will never finally be reducible to an energy source that we can turn on and off at will. He wants us to remember that as God he is great and he reminds us of his greatness by occasionally visiting us and leaving a portion of his power in his wake. Not the kind of energy that wise people jump up and try to snatch like Simon the magician tried to do. But an eternal wave of divine power that reminds us that we are not in the same orbit with God. Something he has that we will never fully possess—only admire and revere—a holy splendor that causes us to sit down quietly and be still and let him get on with being God.

When these great moments leap upon a congregation, it enjoys for a time a theocracy—the complete rule of God. For a while, there seems to be no need for anyone to stand and announce a hymn or turn to a text or open the altar. God takes care of it all. His guidance is so personal that human directions seem out of place and orders of worship useless.

As pastors we relish such moments. They remind us again in visual form what we know to always be true in the realm of the Spirit. Those people whom we are guiding are really not our people at all. They are his. They are the people of God. They do not belong to us. They belong to him. And when he chooses to lead them directly, we are more than happy to sit among the sheep and for a time let him alone be the Shepherd. We are quite willing to walk down his path and sit with our people beside the still waters.

In fact, as the pastors of our congregations, when such events happen, we find ourselves a little unsure of how much or how little to do. Vance Havner used to say that where there is holy fire there is bound to be wild fire, and most of us know the dangers of someone getting out of the Spirit and spoiling the beauty. So we sit poised and alert.

We certainly do not want to intrude on the moment. Nor do we want it to evaporate in a mist of emotion with no lasting value. So we sit with our people at the edge of heaven and listen with all of our powers for the signals from another world. Whatever we do, we have the awesome sense that the moment is so precious that we must treat it with the most delicate care that our fragile minds can muster.

Perhaps the most astounding characteristic of God's penetrating presence in a worship service is the radical changes of behavior that it prompts among our people. Men who never cry stand to praise God and choke back tears which they thought had dried up long ago. Children who are normally rowdy and rude sit like rocks barely moving their heads. People who didn't know they could say "Praise the Lord" out loud and survive the damage to their cool detached image praise the Lord—and survive.

The first time it happened at our church during my pastorate was on a Sunday morning in November. The first clue that something extraordinary was about to happen came in the form of a pesky delay. I was back with the choir waiting for the signal from the organist to enter the sanctuary. The clock on the wall showed four minutes past the hour, and being a stickler for starting service on time, I was getting antsy. Worship services are crammed enough as it is. They certainly don't need a pokey organist who can't find his music to squeeze them any more. As the minutes slipped away, those thoughts were going through my mind. I'm a preacher after all, and preachers are turf conscious. They don't want the sermon crowded at the end.

When the door finally opened, it wasn't a musician at all, but my head usher who stood at the door.

"Pastor, you need to come out here quick. Something wonderful is happening. Three people have testified, and a visiting couple are at the altar to be saved."

I hurried out the door with far less dignity than I had intended, but with way more excitement. The choir did too. There we were, groomed and practiced and ready for the processional, but God had already proceeded. We knew it the instant we entered the sanctuary. That hovering heaviness of God, that mysterious nearness that captures every mind and glues every eye to the next motion of the hand of God.

Nobody scribbled on the tithing envelopes that morning. Nobody dozed off. Nor did anyone act rudely or out of order. God's power lay so thickly around us that we wept and prayed and praised with the tender warmth that God alone deserves. Parents and children whom I had not seen speak for months met in the aisle and stood arm in arm as we sang "Leaning on the Everlasting Arms." Couples who had been stretching each others' patience to the limit knelt at the altar only to stand and embrace and cry. Children sat or stood reverently. Older people waved their hands in long, slow rhythms like grains of ripened wheat in a gentle, summer breeze.

As pastor I checked my watch now and then, but when we finally dismissed at 1:30 P.M. nobody seemed in a hurry to go home. They stayed on, waiting to see if there might be more, if another grand moment of celebration might break into the holy lull.

Such days don't happen often in the life of a congregation, but when they do they have the capacity for redirecting the lives and lifestyles of the entire group. Old struggles which have festered in the church for years can be vanished completely in one holy sweep. Bitter feelings that have prevented growth can be cleared up, never to reappear. Dennis Kinlaw is right. "Give me one divine moment when God acts, and I say that moment is far superior to all the human efforts of man throughout the centuries" (*One Divine Moment*, Robert E. Coleman, Ed., Revell).

The pastor also has cause to celebrate when God's unique radiance marks other occasions as well. Beyond the seasons of blessing in the sanctuary, there are also inspiring times that happen when only two or three are gathered in his name. In these instances the pastor may not be present, but even a testimonial of how God paid a special visit gives way to inner joy.

My friend Della carries with her everywhere she goes a heart pumping with care. When she spots someone whose life has taken a tough turn, she goes to where the hurt is. When our mutual friend, Sarah, lay dying with cancer, Della crowded an already busy schedule with a daily visit to the hospital. Day after day she looked down into Sarah's face, shriveled and gaunt, marked with deep furrows of pain.

"At times," she said, "I would walk down that long corridor in the hospital with waves of anxiety rising in my heart about what I might say to help Sarah today."

One day toward the end of Sarah's life, when she could no longer even force a whisper from her lips, Della climbed into her car and headed for the hospital. As she drove, her mind once again wrestled with the question, "What can I say to Sarah today? What message can I give her that will lift her spirits?"

As she neared the hospital she turned on the car radio and heard Sandi Patti singing "We Shall Behold Him." In a flash the Holy Spirit prompted her, "Tell Sarah that. Tell her that we shall behold him."

Della parked her car and walked into the hospital room that afternoon and without any other introduction, she leaned over close to her dying friend and spoke quietly in her ear. "Sarah, guess what the Holy Spirit gave me to say to you today!"

Sarah could no longer speak, but Della saw a half-wink rise from her eyes.

"He told me to tell you that we shall behold him."

Sarah understood. And in spite of the intense pain she again strained out half a wink. For a quarter of an hour, Della said later, the room was filled with the glory of God. No words were needed. No other signals could have improved on what both of them were feeling together.

"Just the two of us," she said, "enjoying the healing winds of another world."

Several hours later, the phone rang back in Della's office. She picked it up, and Sarah was beholding him.

A pastor friend told of living a similar miraculous moment at, of all places, a board meeting. The church stood at the point of a pivotal decision. They had outgrown the present plant but the dollar pinch had made the building of a new facility seem impossible. Yet the people were willing to venture forward if the pastor felt clearly about it. The pastor described what happened.

> Most of the board members who attended the annual board meeting retreat came assuming that they would be voting to go forward with the new building. Our educational facilities were inadequate and in need of expansion. Two worship services helped deal with the crowding on Sunday mornings.
>
> The retreat began with an extended time of prayer. It was not by coincidence that after a lengthy time of prayer, God began to uniformly change all our minds. One person mentioned that the proposed building would also be inadequate in two years. Another came up with a better way to utilize our present space. I suggested that we get a fix on where we hoped to be at in five-and ten-year intervals. The vote was unanimous and no one was surprised. We voted to wait and do more planning. But we knew that before the vote. How gracious the Lord was that day to give us a double gift of wisdom and joy.

When it comes to ministry, unlike with so many other professions with CEOs, the pastor never calls the final shots. Because he works for God, he is responsible to the higher power. When such awesome surges grip a group of people, the pastor, as at no other time, celebrates that fact. The work he is doing is God's.

When Elijah later shared with Elisha about God's coming to the cave, he would have used a typical word from Old Testament days: *kavod*. The term *kavod* traces back to a root meaning of "heavy." When God came close, the people said that God's presence was "heavy." Today we translate the same word as "glory." When the glory of God falls upon our worship with surging power, we are being biblical to say that God is throwing his weight around, that his presence, heavy with help, is filling the sanctuary.

God alone knows how often to bring his glory—his heavy presence—into our worship. He alone knows when to break into our worship patterns and do something that's not in the bulletin. He doesn't do it often. But with his uncanny sense of timing, he knows just when to bring a holy ambience that solves more problems in a flash than we could humanly handle in a lifetime. As a pastor you might wish for him to be the "heavy weight" a little more often, but you have to trust that he always does it just enough.

In a way far beyond our poor power to finally see, he moves in boldly and sweeps his house clean. When he does, we stand in his wake and speak in whispered tones about a God who could easily thunder in the decibels of a tornado or an earthquake, but more often, as Elijah found, he prefers the gentle whisper of the wind.

7

Rerouting the Exodus

Celebrating Your People's Progress

Wouldn't it be delightful to have a map which showed the exact route of the Exodus? No, not the one in the atlas with the smooth red arrows. I mean the real route with all the zigs and zags marked in—the one that etched in all the detours Moses had to make on the main tour. If he could crack open an atlas today and see how we've ironed out the wrinkles in the route—how we've made it look as simple as an afternoon stroll through a breezy meadow—he would laugh out loud.

Hindsight makes it seem as pleasant as a picnic. Millions of people. Rocks full of water. Dinner on the ground. Family all around. Quail in the air. Clothes that kept their crease. So what else could a body need?

If Moses could only be here to help with our cartography, he would draw things differently. His version of the story would be a shocker. The number of jogs he would mark in the route would drive a mapmaker bent on making a pretty map insane. He would tell about one tribe that hit a streak of independence and struck out on a different course across the mountains. He'd mention stragglers who got lost and held up the whole processional. There would be detours and shortcuts and dead ends, spinning off in all directions. An accurate map of the Exodus, if Moses could draw it, would look more like an explosion than a direction.

If only he could have had a decent spirit of harmony among the travelers, it might not have been so bad. But getting unity out of that bunch must have been a lot like expecting all the fans at a ball game to cheer for the same team. It just didn't happen. Complete harmony about which was the right heading never came. Even with God out in front of everybody in a cloud, Moses still couldn't pull it off.

There he'd be all packed up and ready for another day's journey only to have a messenger come running up, "Hey, Moses, Dan's tribe didn't know you were wanting to leave this early. They still haven't taken their tents down. They wanted to know if we could leave tomorrow." And no sooner would that scout disappear into dust than another would show, "Yo, Moses, a few of the men have been out looking around this morning, and they were wondering if it wouldn't be better to go across the mountain that way. They wanted me to tell you. They said they'd be glad to lead if you wanted them to."

Thanks, wow, thanks, Moses must have thought. *Just what we need—twelve tribes traipsing off in twelve different directions.*

"Oh, Moses!" (Here it came again.) "What's the possibility of taking the scenic route? The ladies think the sunset will be prettier from over there!"

And in-between complaints about the route, the food got into the discussion.

"Moses, what's the option on this quail? Dark bland or white bland? And this manna? Could you see if God could send it in flavors? This vanilla is getting old. At least back in Egypt we had a choice. Could we go back?"

Moses had heard it all. Go forward. Go sideways. Go back. And if somebody had thought of it, go up.

As we sit here today high on the hilltop of history look-ing back those thousands of years, the Exodus conjures up images of endurance and triumph, harmony and pride. However, for a man named Moses, standing at the front of that motley mass of opinions on the dusty floor of the Wilderness of Zin, the trip must have seemed like anything but a journey of joy.

As hair raising as the march through the Red Sea must have been, it probably seemed like a 100-yard dash com-pared with the marathon of agonizing drudgery that stretched ahead. If he had been picking, there must have been days when Moses would have taken four or five Red Seas over one of the weary journeys afterward. The wilder-ness must have at times seemed endless, the dust suffocat-ing, the obstacles eternal. If Moses had only known how long it would take and how arduous the task, you wonder if he would have ever started out at all.

The amazing miracle of the Exodus is not that it got started. The people were anxious to leave. The miracle of the Exodus is that it finally ended. After years of meander-ing all over the wilderness and bleaching their bones in the sweltering desert sun, the people finally arrived. Canaan came into view. Thirty-eight years and about seven hun-dred miles more than they needed to go, they at long last reached their destination. The miracle of the parting of the Red Sea is nothing to sneeze at, but that the people ever made it all the way to Canaan is the greatest miracle of all. When they finally stood at the edge of the Jordan and dipped their toes in the churning stream, that is the picture which above all others tells us that the Exodus was an act of God. By no other means could a group of people so fickle and fidgety have gotten that far in one piece.

A look at your church is like seeing the Exodus revis-ited. If you only had to get people converted and leave it at that, it might not be so bad. But once you've gotten them out of Egypt and through the Red Sea, that long stretch of wilderness is still ahead. Most of us would do cartwheels on the church lawn if conversion solved all of a person's problems and rendered them promptly mature. Wouldn't it be terrific if on one Sunday you could see them in the slough of sin and the next standing in front of a Sunday school class explaining the several levels of love in the Gospel of John. But wildernesses are long things. The fight against sin is so everlastingly daily. Once the hurdle of conversion is passed, the venture of faith is only begun.

Those of us who have coaxed and cajoled and pulled and tugged to keep people moving along spiritually feel a special attachment to Moses. His lot is a lot like ours. If you are called to be a leader for God, you may as well settle in for the long haul and decide to celebrate the steps of progress all along the way. If you insist on holding off on the party until the work is finished, you'll probably never party at all. The key to contentment in ministry is to learn to enjoy the slender gains and the gradual growth and the lurchy advances. Frankly it is amazing that our people with all the welter of ways open to them ever find the right one at all. That they ever sort it out and stick with it at all is a miracle, no matter what their level of love for Christ.

When your thoughts turn to praising your people for their progress, there are several avenues down which to travel. Probably nothing is quite so simultaneously frustrating and fantastic about the people in your congregation as the fact that they each have a free will. Born into every one of them is an inalienable right to pick and choose as they please. When it comes to right and wrong, you can point and prod and push, but in the end they have a mind of their own. They may have left the bondage of sin behind, but at times they sure don't seem in any hurry to get much beyond that. They dawdle and backslide and flirt with the old ways to the point of spiritual jeopardy. And all the while you watch with one eye and close the other in prayer. If only they'd make a clean break and not only step away from sin, but get far enough away so it couldn't entice them back.

A newspaper article described a family of three that stepped into a street cafe in New York City one evening for dinner. The waitress showed them to a booth and stepped back to the kitchen while the three of them, a father and mother and their seven-year-old son, studied the menu.

After a few minutes she returned with pencil and pad and proceeded to take their orders. The mother ordered roast beef, green beans, potatoes, and a roll. The father also ordered a well-balanced and tasty meal. Then the waitress turned to the little boy.

"And what will you have, sonny?"

He glanced at his father.

"A hamburger," he started, "I want a hamburger. . . ."

And both parents barked at once.

"No, you won't have a hamburger. You're going to eat good food. No more of this junk food in your stomach." They sounded serious.

As soon as they had finished their speech, the waitress turned to the little boy again.

"And what will you have on your hamburger, sonny?"

His eyes bugged wider.

"Ketchup, please, lots of ketchup. And bring me some fries and a Coke."

"Coming right up." And before the stunned parents could recover and figure out what to say, the lady had disappeared behind the swinging doors into the kitchen. When she was out of earshot, the little boy looked up at his parents.

"Hey, Dad, Mom, guess what? That lady thinks I'm real."

As a pastor we win by remembering that God takes every person in our pews for real. If they want to eat spiritual junk food or stay on milk way past their spiritual infancy, they can. No matter how good or poor their spiritual choices, they are uniquely real. And really in our better moments we wouldn't have it any other way. Suppose you could by your own human authority demand that people shape up or get out. Suppose you could rap them on the knuckles and force them to eat at your pace and grow at your speed. You might get growth, but there would also come a sad cheapening of their own free spirit—a terrible squelching of their innate ability to embrace a course of their own. There would be something pitiful about a soul free to soar no higher than the level of shoelaces, bound by the tether of another struggling spirit.

So we celebrate their independence, their power to pick their own destiny. They may decide to do it "my way" or they may choose to go "God's way," but whatever their choice, our higher happiness must rest, not in the fact that they followed through on our directions, but that they out of their own free will chose to take the higher road. If God believes in them that much, if he trusts them with their choices in spite of the risk, so should we. We may at times feel that like the runners in *Alice in Wonderland*—they had no starting point and certainly no destination. We might wish they would take advantage of more of the wisdom of previous generations and go fast forward in faith, but something there is about every generation of Christians that they want to touch his hands and thrust their finger in his side for themselves.

As a child growing up, I loved to watch westerns, especially when the cowboys set out to corral a herd of wild mustangs. I didn't exactly know why, but I got excited when I saw those horses running wild. Every time one of them escaped the noose and galloped arrogantly back across the range, I'd clap and yell and celebrate that those bad, old cowboys had missed again. At least one proud spirit was still free.

After becoming a pastor, I still thrill when a stallion breaks free, but I don't clap as loudly as before. The parable is too sharp, the lesson too clear. Still I revel in the independence of my people. In the end I shall not have to answer for them. I can lead them to the edge of heaven, but whether or not they decide to visit there is a matter strictly their own.

I'm always glad when they desire to accept my teaching and follow my suggestions, but I admire their free will too much to ever think that unless they go my way they will always be going the wrong way. I may some day meet the happy surprise that a few of the paths that I tried to keep them from going down were really the best routes after all. One pastor framed the feeling in these words:

> Some of my deepest feelings of satisfaction come from knowing that I am going through life with my people. My years of pastoral work with one congregation have allowed me to experience the total range of their individual and family dramas: birth, dreams, celebrations, traumas, illnesses and death, and the kaleidoscope of all the other events shaping them in the seasons of life. The experience of living life with my people is the most important thing I do in terms of being a part of this local family of God.

The editor of the *Timberlake Monthly* described his visit to the giant sequoias in California. The guide had pointed out to the group that the sequoia tree has roots that reach only slightly below the surface. He had reacted. "That's impossible! I'm a country boy, and I know that if the roots don't grow deep into the earth, strong winds will blow the trees over."

"Not sequoia trees," said the guide. "They grow only in groves and their roots intertwine under the surface of the earth. So when the strong winds come, they hold each other up."

There's our lesson to learn. Our people are a lot like the giant sequoias. They may not be very deep as individuals, but together they hold each other up. Together they make a pretty strong stand.

When it comes to praising progress, there is also a time for relishing the fact that not all the spiritual growth in our congregation happens in a straight line, not all maturity comes about because our people got new insights on how to live and put them into practice right away. Much growth happens in the roundabout way.

There is a tendency to equate slow and lurchy growth with a weaker finish. If a person doesn't mature in a steady straight line, we have a suspicion that they may not be growing at all.

I have often imagined how delightful it would be if the people in my congregation dressed according to their spiritual maturity. There they would sit on Sunday morning, a few of them in three-piece suits, but a good number of them in diapers, cooing and shaking their bottles. Others would be in overalls and boots, ready for the hard work ahead. The scene would be a marvelous surprise. But even the ones in diapers would be a step removed from total nudity. And with everyone sitting around peeping, even diapers would be a welcomed sight.

In the church of my childhood there was a man who set the record for rededicating his life to Christ. About once a year at special renewal services he would arrive at the altar, weeping and vowing that he was now ready to make the commitment of a lifetime. For about a month after he'd arrive to worship thirty minutes early and sit on the front pew. As the pastor preached, he would nod his head and lift his hand and any visitor to the service would have sworn that he had been living close to Christ since the crib. But sometime during the second month, you'd catch him sitting three or four pews back. His head wouldn't nod quite as often and everybody knew what was up. Uncle Frank was on a slide. By the end of six months he'd be slumped on the back pew, barely looking up, and before the year was out, on Sunday mornings Uncle Frank would be at home. As children we used to test our prophetic abilities by guessing how long it would take Uncle Frank to make it to the back pew.

When the pastor would try to intercept his regression, Uncle Frank would just say, "Well, Pastor, it's a little something that gets me down spiritually, but I don't feel free to talk about it right now." So year after year Uncle Frank would draw near to God only to slip back time after time.

As he got older he changed. Nobody knows how it happened, but everyone is thrilled that it did. Somewhere along the way, Frank found a firmer grip on his faith and the pew changing came to an end. He neither sat right on the front nor did he move to the back. He finally found a permanent seat about two-thirds of the way to the front and from then until his death he was the picture of consistency.

To say that Uncle Frank's faith was inferior to another person who never went through his fluctuations would be unfair. His strength of will may not have matched that of others, but the fact that it took him a longer time to arrive at a pattern of steady devotion says nothing at all about how strong his love for Christ really was. He may have come along by leaps and spurts and sputters, but he was as deeply in love with Christ as anyone in our church.

Frank's case is a classic example of why ministry is so difficult to measure in the short stretch. A single year is not nearly long enough to tell the story of our people's growth in God. A few in our church believed in instant holiness and neat crisp breaks with sin, so they wrote Frank off as a hopeless case. But several others insisted that for him progress was not so much the bound of a single day as the call of a lifetime, so they kept the encouragement flowing. Over time Frank proved they were right.

People who accept the Christian faith and never look back may be less work for us as pastor, but those who flounder toward their futures merit our applause too, for in both instances, they are moving in the direction of God.

Try It

Take a moment to transfer the concept of consistency over to your call to the ministry. For many pastors the call comes clearly and neatly. One moment it's absent and the next it's there, full-blown from the start. For many others, the call is a gradually unfolding certainty. It begins with small hunches and hints and concludes over time with a maturing confidence.

But if the hardliners were reviewing your call in its early stages, would they have kept you or culled you? If they had been scrutinizing you as a young minister on the basis of confidence and natural ability and consistency, would you have passed the test?

Perhaps all beginnings need to be enveloped in more patience. Whether they are the beginnings of Christian faith, or a call to ministry, or a marriage, or parenting, they may need more time than we are by nature inclined to give them. When we expect too much too soon we may be jeopardizing a successful future because of a fledgling start. A reminder to ourselves and to other more mature people is often helpful in letting us know again that a lot of our beginnings weren't all that astonishing either. And some of our more mature work could still probably stand a touch of improvement.

During a walk in the woods, it is quite common to see a tree that has grown around a pasture fence, completely enclosing it in its growth. For a while the fence had blocked its way and scraped away its life. But in time by persistent growth, it overcame the barrier and even grasped it to make it a part of its upward expansion. In the life of the soul, growth is also often stymied and progress slowed. But what we see and cheer again and again is the picture of a man who faces the barriers of life, and instead of giving up, steps on and over the barrier, using it to his advantage as he goes slowly on his way.

There is another sidepath to this truth about progress. It is also true, that depending on your point of view, your people's staggered progress can be either an agony or a joy. No matter what the church, there will always be sprawling differences in the people's pace of progress. Moses must have experienced it. That group of people, walking in the wilderness, far from forming a tight side-by-side line of march, were strung out farther than his eyes could see. One tribe would invariably be up and ready to go, while another would loiter as though they were thinking of settling down. At any given moment, several would be falling farther and farther behind, while another group would be getting farther and farther ahead. While one group was anxious to go, another would be voting to stay, and all in the middle the largest crowd wouldn't know whether to go or stay. So up and down the line he'd go, barking orders for one group to cool it and hold back and coaxing another to get on the move.

During my days as a collegian, I spent one summer painting houses. There were six of us in the painting club altogether, and when the call came, we would descend on a house and in less than a day we could transform a dreary skeleton of a house into a dazzling white mansion that rivaled the Taj Mahal.

Along with my painting I did a lot of looking. I'd watch the other fellows at their jobs. Three of them had just come from other painting experiences and their practice showed. They'd whip out a bucket and a brush and swish that paint back and forth without losing a single drop. Those guys could have worn their suits and gone straight on to church afterward, and nobody would have had the slightest hint where they had been all day.

But the other three of us were in a different league—the minor league. I distinctly remember the day I started down one side of an exterior wall and by the time I finished (and three-and-a-half gallons later), two of the boxwoods under the window were the exact same color as the wall. I learned later that Sherwin-Williams had invented a hook to hold the bucket on a ladder, but I had come upon the invention too late.

The other two guys in my category were equally clumsy. One of them spent more time tipping his brush to see if he could keep it from dripping than he did wiping the paint on the wall. The other one had a gift for creating rivers of paint on window sills, which in turn flowed down the side of the wall and fanned out into a delta before dropping on the ground below. The delta near the drip was the thing I admired. What delighted me most of all about the job was that all six of us got exactly the same pay. I am sure the three professionals had passing hunches of being cheated, but the other three of us felt like we had struck a pretty fair deal.

In the church we also work with a group of people whose talents and commitments run the full compass. We sing "Onward, Christian soldiers, marching as to war" as if we had a troop of people marching briskly forward shoulder to shoulder toward the Promised Land. But unless your church is highly unusual, it would be truer to life to sing "Onward, Christian stragglers, wobbling off to war." In spite of their love for God, they are still strikingly human and in all likelihood will remain so for a long time to come. As a pastor you must take delight in the fact that they are moving. At different speeds, yes—but they *are* moving. And no matter how many times you have to run up and down the line, scolding one and applauding another, the trend is definitely onward. As one pastor put it, "They are training in the liturgy of life." When you pause to back up and look at your life, you will be amazed again at how God can take such an unlikely group of people and move them all persistently forward.

Another cause for perpetual praise lies in the truth that much of the growth in a congregation happens unseen. That is why ministry is so difficult to measure. In describing a weeping willow you might say that it shades an area forty feet across, that its trunk is rather smooth, its leaves slender, its branches green. But if that weeping willow is standing at the edge of a lake with its sweeping branches cascading down to meet their equally beautiful reflection in the water, a description won't do it. You have to see it for yourself.

In ministry we only see a part of the progress; we only get a piece of the picture. There is a whole kaleidoscope of care that we never see. During the week our people become a moving mass of love, a roving host of Good Samaritans, but we never see it all. They go out to drape other people's burdens across their own shoulders and in most cases lay them down before we get a chance to see it.

Without ever notifying us at all, the Holy Spirit marches through our communities and taps the talents of our people and completes a ministry and never returns to mark it

in our memory. Then again when we least expect it, a passing comment will stab us wide awake again to the fact that
we aren't getting all the signals clear, even of what we do
see. Recently a man in my congregation caught me completely off guard. He's the kind of person who gives the
impression of being completely numb, oblivious to every
stimuli in his environment. On more than one occasion I
had wondered to myself why he even came to church. You
could never tell by watching him if he loved it or hated it,
or if he even knew anything was going on. He's one of
those guys who, even when he is present, you still wonder
if he's fully there.

But one Sunday morning he came up after the service
and bowled me over. "Hey, Pastor, this series you've been
giving us, it's really helping me and my wife. We've
noticed the clear connection among all the messages and
we're talking about your thoughts way into the night."
"Wow, terrific, super!" (He had no idea how stunned I
was.) "That's wonderful, David. I'm glad to be of help."
Boy, was I ever! I had no idea any of that stuff was getting
under the lid. When I left the church that morning, I nearly
strutted. If David was getting something out of it, I was
definitely on the roll.

On trips that last long as ministry, you have to make a
commitment to be content along the way. A commitment
to contentment doesn't mean that you are always happy
with the pace of progress, nor even pleased with your own
leadership. But it does mean that you are not baffled every
time your people take a detour from your plan. Perhaps
after all there's a lesson down the sidepath that they could
never get by moving unveeringly behind you. Perhaps
their very humanness demands that they occasionally
challenge your plan and point off to another place. Perhaps
for inner release we need to accept the advice of George
Mickelson, governor of South Dakota, in his blurb on the
back of a South Dakota map. "A map," he suggests, "can
take you just about anywhere, but for a memorable trip
you really ought to know when to fold it up and put it

aside. Because one of the best ways to travel is to get a little bit lost, literally and on purpose."

So your people sometimes stray from your infallible plan. So they get a little bit lost on purpose. That's no reason to crumple your vision and toss it aside. What if Moses had done that? What if he had cancelled Canaan the first or even the second time one of the tribes defied his goal?

Part of the reason we celebrate Moses as a great leader is that he was able to weave all their little strategies into his great strategy. He had Canaan in mind, and despite all the energies that pulled in every other direction, he stuck to his vision. At every point along the way he found himself disentangling his people from the old habits of a lifetime, but as messy as that got at times, he refused to let it mire him up and bury his dream. He was on his way somewhere and his grip on the goal only got stronger as he moved.

There's a tinge of sadness in the biblical account of the Exodus. After forty years of guiding a mass of humanity through a vast and broiling desert; after enduring rounds of criticism and resolving a ton of disputes, Moses never entered the Promised Land. He saw it. But it was another man who took the people in. He had planted and he had watered, but it was Joshua who saw the increase.

But I can't believe for a moment that Moses sat on Mount Nebo, pouting. There he was now, an older man, his days of leadership behind him. But there he stands on the side of that mountain, his eyes scanning that beautiful land of Canaan which he had lived and dreamed and breathed for forty years. And the only picture I can draw of him as he stands there in his last grand moment as patriarch is one of celebration. His people stand in the valley below; the new leader is already in place. But just before God attends to his funeral arrangements, Moses stands there pointing toward Canaan and clapping. Tears are brimming in his eyes. He can see it now. He can see the land that he had seen so often through the eye of faith. So he stands and points and claps. He will never put his foot on the land himself. But his people will, and that's what counts. Joshua will and that's just fine. There's no way he's going to his grave a moping man. He had brought them this far by faith. There is the prize all before him and there are his people standing next to it. And when Moses finally closed his eyes and lay down to sleep his longest sleep, a smile as wide as the wilderness and as lovely as the Jordan must have been playing across his face.

8

Standing in the Gap

Celebrating Your Successes

Ezekiel had seen it many times. Living as he did in the war-ravaged world of Palestine, he had seen again and again an enemy army come roaring down the mountain to pounce on an unsuspecting village in the valley. Dozens of people would be massacred, homes would be pillaged, food supplies devoured. It was the kind of picture that caused the blood to boil: helpless people retreating for their lives, only to run into another wave of soldiers behind them as they tried to flee. The blood flowed freely. And Ezekiel had seen it and hated it.

How could a small town full of innocent people ever stand against so great an army? How could a safety wall built around the city be kept solid, when battering rams were being slammed against it from every side? As he watched the carnage, anger and pity vied for control of his soul.

In all his life Ezekiel had only seen one corrective for the terrible injustice, and it had been extremely risky. One day as he stood watching a tiny town take it on the chin from a bullying army, he saw with sadness the soldiers rip a gap-

119

ing hole in the safety wall. In just moments he knew that
the news would spread among the troops that the wall had
been ruptured, and they would swarm the breach and
storm the town. But as he watched he could hardly believe
the sudden twist of plot. A lone man from the town
grabbed his sword and dropped down right in the middle
of the crumbled rocks at the rupture and began swinging
wildly as if he thought a one-man militia could save the
town. No sooner had he made the leap than a dozen other
men fell in beside him. Their raw courage and vicious defi-
ance stunned the attackers. Convinced that they had
walked into a human hornet's nest, the army beat a hasty
retreat and left the little village to repair its wall and get on
with life. And all because one man risked his life and stood
in the gap.

If Ezekiel could sit looking over the cities and towns of
our day, the scene would seethe the heart with pain again.
He would see enemies of a far more subtle and sinister
nature attacking and ravaging the minds of our people.
And he would also see a man or woman at every wall
dropping right in the middle of the gap to parry the
assault of the enemy. The work is risky, but it is a normal
part of the pastor's job. It is at once his danger and his
delight to stand in between his people and the swirling
whirl of subtle demons waiting to pounce in and destroy
them. And in closing the spiritual gap, he must work in
two directions: he must not only fend off Satan, he must at
the same time draw his people nearer to God.

Closing the gap between your people and God demands
a will to keep at it even when the number of things going
wrong outnumber the things going right. Very few people
have the privilege of working with so many variables that
can so suddenly cluster in reverse or converge in progress.
As a matter of course the pastor deals with volunteer com-
mittees, assistant pastors, worship leaders, and board
members, who along with him struggle with their own
spiritual disciplines. Spiritual zealots demand that he force
all members to be as spiritual as they are. A few people on

the fringe of the church's life are sure their nod to God will be enough. And of course you have your own changing moods to manage as you walk alongside your people on the way to God.

As children we used to play at a game which is a child's parable for ministry. About five or six BBs were enclosed under a plastic bubble on the top of a card. The trick was to get a BB in each of the holes on the card all at the same time. It might be a picture of a baseball diamond with a BB per base or an apple tree with BB apples. But whatever the picture, the game could be tormenting. Just as you tipped the card enough to roll one BB near the hole, another one would pop out and there you'd be back at hole one. On more than one occasion I remember flinging the card down in disgust. Why couldn't they have put a drop of glue in the hole to keep the silly BB in place once it landed? As an eight-year-old I had no idea that the small plastic card would someday be my parish and that the BBs would be alive.

In ministry, if you keep on top of it all, you simply have to decide to see and savor partial progress and almost closures and near hits. You have to believe that the best things in the realm of the Spirit take long stretches of time to set in order. And you have to accept your own rounds of fatigue as part and parcel of the process.

So you only get 40-percent cooperation when you ask your people to sponsor the local community cleanup. Hey, that's 40 percent better than 0 percent! So you celebrate the 40 percent; or you delegate a job with a deadline to your vice chairman, only to discover that two days before it's due, it's not done. And you swallow hard in disbelief and do it yourself. In ministry, as in all other professions, you have to keep looking at the white page and not the dark spots on it. Otherwise you'll get disenchanted, put out, mad. Try to lead people in one direction, and they zigzag off down every path but the right path. Try to help them love and one or two will keep on hating no matter how often you highlight the great commandment. Urge them to be friendly to visitors, and someone will still catch the newcomer at the door and say, "We're glad you're here today. Your children made a lot of noise in children's church, but we're still glad you came."

As one woman told her pastor, "Pastor, it's not that I've lost my faith. It's just that I'm not living it." If you sat down to sum up your successes in ministry you would need to sprinkle in a large number of phrases like "almost but not quite," "firmly planted in midair," "halfhearted help," "close but no cigar," and "lurching awkwardly forward."

Try It

Take this quiz and see where you rank. Assign each sentence a number between one and ten. If you mark a ten, you are saying that you performed that task or accomplished that goal exactly the way you wanted to. If you put a five, you are saying that you feel you did about average, and if you put a one, you are thinking of your behavior in that area a total flop. Assign a number to each of the following.

How well did I do this week on:
1. The number of hours I like to spend on my sermon and the hours I actually spent?
2. The balance I struck between my church work and my family time?
3. The effectiveness of my pastoral calls? Did I accomplish what I went there to do?
4. Staying organized? Did I stay on top of things and finish tasks on time?
5. Attending to my personal spiritual formation? This does not count the time I spent working at the church or preparing another sermon. It has to do with how I did in caring for my own soul.
6. My reading? Did I stimulate my mind with new thoughts which can help to deepen my teaching and preaching?
7. Responding to unexpected developments? These include such things as late-night calls to the hospital, resolving con-

flicts between people or dealing with an angry creditor who claims that the church is delinquent in its payments.
8. Attending to the needs of my body? Did I get enough sleep and exercise?
9. Relaxing? Did the strain of my work spill over into my day off (if you take one)? Did I get a decent break this week?
10. Enjoying what I'm doing? Have I enjoyed this week, or has it been a hard and dull chore?

Total up your score. If your total is in the fifty range, you are typical of people in ministry in your self-evaluation. If you scored seventy or better, you need to start counting your blessings and if you gave yourself a ninety, you need to ask God to let whatever is happening to you last a long, long time.

Ministry requires a funny fusion. It requires you to praise and prod at the same time. You have to lift people up, while at the same time bearing down. You have to insert the needle and be ready with the salve in the other hand. You must cheer but you must also chide. The truth you proclaim hurts—but it also heals. You appreciate how far they have come, but at the end of a long day, you are overwhelmed at how far they still need to go.

One day Bill, a pastor in Michigan, responded to a knock at his front door. A man who looked to be about thirty-five-years old stood there in faded jeans and a T-shirt.

"Are you the pastor of the church over there?" The man pointed behind him.

"Yes," Bill responded.

"Could I talk to you for a moment?"

Bill said that his first impulse was to say no. He had met his quota of bums who wanted a free handout from the church and nothing more. But in spite of his feelings, he also felt a hunch to invite the man in.

"Sure, come on in."

The man came in and sat on the front edge of the couch,

while Bill sat down in a chair a few feet away. He fixed his eyes right on Bill and got straight to his story.

"Reverend," he said, "for all but seven years of my life I have lived behind bars. I've been the rounds. First in the detention home, then a reformatory, and for the past several years in the penitentiary. I've been in them all.

"One night, Reverend, I sat in my jail cell planning a way to end it all. I sat there full of hate and fear. I couldn't take it any longer. I thought I was losing my mind. I had never asked God for anything, but in that final desperate hour I looked up at the ceiling of my cell and said, 'God, if you can help me, do it.'

"Reverend, I instantly felt a power come into that cell and fill my body. It got so intense that I started yelling at the top of my lungs. A couple of guards came running down the hall to see what was happening. They called in a doctor, but he couldn't find anything wrong with me. Finally they called in the chaplain. We talked about half an hour, then he looked at me and said, 'John, you've been converted to Christ. As far as I can tell, you've experienced a sudden salvation.'

"I believe he was right, Reverend. I knew I was a different man. I started reading everything I could about God. I read all the books about God that they had in the jail. I had books brought in from the public library. I had never been in a church in my life, but the chaplain said they might have books on God, so I called around and had books brought in from churches. But, Reverend, the book I have read the most is the Book of Acts. I have read it over and over.

"About a year after my conversion in the jail cell, I got a message from the warden's office. They said that because of good behavior, I had been recommended for early release. It came the next day and I walked out a free man.

"For the past seven months now I have been hitchhiking up and down the country looking for that church I read about in the Book of Acts. And I can't find it. In that book, Reverend, those people stuck together like a bunch of thieves. They lived together and helped each other and cared like blazes about each other. And I'm not expecting a bunch of people running around in robes and sandals. But every place I've been the people will hardly speak to me. So I'm here to ask you, Reverend, is your church that church in the Book of Acts? Do your people live like they live in that book?"

Bill said, "I sat there stunned. I had never in my life faced the question that abruptly and head-on. I knew I couldn't honestly say yes. But I didn't want to say no. I felt defensive and sad. I mumbled some sort of an answer and invited the man to check out our church for himself the next Sunday. But he was on his way to a prison in the south and couldn't stay. When the man left," said Bill, "I put my face in my hands and wept. The question had struck deep in my heart. It stayed with me late into the night and into the next day and week. I built a sermon series around it. I entitled it by the question from the man on the couch, 'Is our church that church in the Book of Acts?'

"As time went on," Bill continued, "our church never fully reached the ideal, but the man's question from the couch became the prominent prodding question that dominated all our plans and prayers as we mapped out our direction for the future."

Every pastor must grapple with the balance. He always wants his people to do more and be like those people in the Book of Acts, but he is wise if he relishes what they are already doing and what they've already done. In many ways he has already helped them close the gap between themselves and God, and that progress needs to be noted.

As pastors we fill out our annual reports and drop them in the mailbox, fully aware that most of what we did over the past year didn't get in the record. In the official report we noted the number of times we stood in our pulpit. We made a stab at telling how many people came to know Christ as a result of our ministry. We recorded our loyalty to the denomination by checking the box marked YES by the question, "Did you read the official denominational publications?" We highlighted a book that had been spiritually uplifting for us over the year. This year I put down Paul Sherer's book *The Word God Sent*. We are always asked about our contribution to the church and we fill in the space well aware that we could have given more.

But as the report drops in the mail slot, we have a grand inner satisfaction that much more happened in our ministry than we could ever get into a report. Not even the tip of the story ever gets inside that manila envelope. Much of our inner thrill comes from the fact that the areas where we probably made the most difference will only be known to God.

I think about that couple that came in for counseling, their marriage on the brink. Hour after tense hour they sat in front of me, grasping for a small plot of common ground on which to rebuild their crumbling relationship. We spent long and stressful hours dealing with feelings and tracking down motives. Occasionally their anger would boil over, and I would bow my head and wait and pray and wonder if there was any use wasting any more time on them.

Then a few Sundays ago, when I saw them walk down the aisle with their new baby, and sit down with her parents as if there had never been a ripple, I sat on the platform with a jubilee dancing in my soul. During one of the hymns, I caught Todd's eye and winked. He nodded slightly and winked in return. I thought how terrific it was that in spite of all the onlookers, he and I could still have our private moment of celebration. Only he and I knew how much was being communicated in that wink. The report in the mailbox didn't say anything about Todd and Becky, but I filed it in my heart. Their rebonding was the stuff reports ought to be made of. But I left it out because it didn't quite fit any of the categories. Still it was one of the highlights of that year of ministry, and I reported it again to my soul. Not every marriage-counseling session that year had met with success, but that one had, and I felt honored to be part of the healing.

Nor did I include anything in my report about Marlene. Her death did raise the number in the necrology column by one, but that stroke of the pen said nothing at all about that woman's majestic last days.

Marlene and I had met five years before in the nursing home, her face twisted by far more than age. She hated her family, especially her children, and the anger in her heart only warped her physical features that much more. At first she treated me with deadly venom. Her long years of fighting with her children had built up one of the most bitter spirits I had seen in all my ministry.

Then one night Marlene took a turn for the worse. As soon as the nurse had called, I dropped everything to be by her side. Her children were afraid to come around for fear that their coming would only aggravate her condition. So I sat and watched and listened. Hour after hour I absorbed the hostility and scorn as it poured from her shrunken lips. At the end of every meeting, I would squeeze her hand and say, "Marlene, your life has been hard, but I love you. You're a beautiful woman inside, and I love you."

She always acted gruff and shrugged off my concern. But every time I insisted on getting in the last word, "Marlene, I love you, and you're a beautiful woman on the inside."

One day after I had been to the nursing home more times than I could remember she said to me, "Pastor, you handle me pretty well, don't you?"

"I certainly try," I replied. "But, Marlene, I want you to know how serious I am about all this care and love and stuff. You're my friend."

As her situation deteriorated, I kept drawing closer and closer to the time for asking her to let Christ be a part of her life.

On that particular day I came into the nursing home alone as usual. Marlene was sitting in the chair by her bed, moaning softly in pain.

"Marlene," I awakened her gently, "Marlene, it's good to see you today. How are you feeling?" She mentioned the pain in her chest and arms. I listened and watched as she pointed to the places where her body was hurting. When she finished describing her haunting pain, we sat for a long while, neither of us making a sound. Finally I leaned over toward her and said, "Marlene, I've been your friend for a long time, and I have a little favor to ask of you."

"I know, you want me to forgive my children, don't you?"

I was surprised by her quick reaction.

"Well, that would be nice, but that wasn't exactly what I had in mind."

"Well, let's have it then. What do you want?" Her tone was still cool, but a distinct sense of warmth was beginning to show around the edge.

"Marlene, you've lived a long and full life, but would you do me a favor and let Jesus walk with you the rest of the way?"

She smiled a little as if she suspected that I might get around to that point sometime.

"You know how I hurt and how I hate my children."

"Yes, but the first thing I'd like for you to do is to ask Jesus to walk with you during these difficult days." She paused for a while before responding. I prayed.

"Well, you've been awfully good to me, and for your sake I guess I'm willing to give it a try." At least Marlene was candid. She would do it for my sake. I spent a few moments explaining to her what I thought walking with Jesus would mean for her. Then I asked her to pray. I shall never forget the pointed frankness of Marlene's prayer.

"Dear God, as far as I know I have never talked to you before about helping me with my life. But for this dear man's sake, I am here asking your help. If you want me, I want you. Amen."

It was over almost as soon as it started. At the end when she touched my hand and gave a faint glimmer of a smile, I was sure that Marlene had spoken directly and seriously with God.

After several more conversations, I challenged Marlene

to open lines of communication and forgiveness with her family. She trusted me so much now, that she promised to try that as well. She must have also had a sense that her time for leaving the world was drawing near. Within a two-week-period she called her three children and several other relatives to ask forgiveness for her harsh and bitter spirit. With each phone call a growing pall of peace spread across her face. She was going down fast now, but she was clearly enjoying what Paul spoke of when he wrote, "Though outwardly we are wasting away, yet inwardly we are being renewed day by day" (2 Cor. 4:16).

At Marlene's funeral the three children, two sons and a daughter, stood by her casket with their hands folded on their mother's hands. The daughter spoke for all of them. "Mother was a more lovely woman than she ever let on. Here at the end she finally let the real person show through."

In the eulogy I described Marlene's final expression as she began to catch her breath in heaven's world. Her eyes had looked right at me for a while, then off to my right as if she were looking at something beyond. She never looked back.

Marlene's final hours were filled with joy and family. She had died full of life. The one extra mark in the NUMBER DECEASED column seemed too small a mark for such a triumphant end. But God had already filed the report, and I celebrated the fact that I had watched it being written.

Try It

Just before you drop your next annual report in the mail, reflect on the number of facts that you *didn't* put in it. Think about the questions it doesn't ask. Questions like these: *What was your greatest heartbreak over this past year? What was the greatest miracle in which you were involved? When were you at your lowest spiritually over the year, and what do you think contributed to that? Who gave you the most criticism and was there anything to what they said? How is your church a little better off this year than it was a year ago? How is it worse? Do you really believe in your people? Are they further along in their*

faith than they were a year ago? How many times during the
year did you think about throwing in the towel and getting into a
profession where you could make more money and take less heat?

Every ministry has its "Marlenes." But not all the gaps
we seek to close for God end up with such beautiful healing. On the average we are more likely to get partial results
and tentative closures. In our quest for success in ministry
we occasionally run into nasty obstacles. In fact the number of things that can go wrong on a single day can stagger
the mind. And if you add the backlog of other issues need-
ing attention, you can change what might have been
another unfinished symphony into an outright catastro-
phe.

If you could only go a full week with everything you
nailed down staying down, it would be blissful. But the
very nature of ministry is to have a few things falling apart
while a few more things are finally fitting.

Probably all of us in the ministry have had the thought
at some time or the other that we would like to worship for
a while in a church where we didn't know anybody. We
could just sit there and soak it up and not know a single
sordid story about a person around us. We could get to
God without being distracted by a crowd of ugly memories barging in to push us away.

But after a few weeks, our hearts would draw us back to
the people we know. The air would be too artificial, too
thick with make-believe. The prayers and Scripture reading would remind us that God did not come to help a
whole world; he came to help a broken world. And as his
helpers we ought to keep to our broken world too. So back
we'd go to the partial tithers and Sunday Christians, and
jealous husbands at our own church. We'd go back to those
people who think we are a moving wailing wall and who
need us at every hour except the office hours.

The little boy asked his father more than he knew. "Hey,
Dad," he said, "when did Spot and Wrinkle stop coming to
our church?"

"What do you mean?"

"I heard them singing, 'Tis a glorious church without spot and wrinkle.'"

But the pastor who has lived and loved his people for years knows the real truth. It's a glorious church even *with* spot and wrinkle.

As a leader, your happiness centers in the fact, not that you have a spic-'n'-span church, but that you are working with a cross section of regular people who are both bland and beautiful. For every one that is colorless and dull, there are two others who keep putting the deep-rich burgundy back into life. For every backslider, there's a zealot, and for both of them you are a man sent from God.

One pastor compared the people in his church to a wet bar of soap. If you extend your arm and hold a wet bar of soap you have to be careful. If you hold it too loosely, it will slither out and fall to the ground. If you squeeze it too tightly, it may well squirt up and out the top of your hand. The trick is in the grip.

Sometimes you preach on a truth that your people need to have only one person think you came on too strong while another is tempted to say "Sic 'em." You'll visit a home and see off-color "literature" lying around the house and wonder if the family even heard your message on controlling the mental intake. Apparently if they heard it, they didn't hear it very well or they would have cleaned up their reading right away, or at least stuffed it under the couch before you entered the room.

Ministry is a land of surprises. And perhaps what surprises us the most is the deep belief that God keeps planting in our hearts that if we keep at it, someday most of the problems will be solved, and most of the people saved, and most of the growing done. It is a divine notion, and one of the clearest indicators that we have of the divine nature of our call. With anything less than a divine thrust, we would soon give up. But with God's thumb pressing in our backs and his power surging in our heart, we go on in a spirit of eternal optimism.

The pastor of a rural congregation summed it up like this:

> In ministry, as in farming, there is a time of preparation, a time of planting, watering and cultivating before a harvest can be expected. I have to admit, there are times when I grow weary of waiting on the harvest. Often I labor for long periods of time and see no apparent results. But then the joy of the harvest comes when I see or hear someone responding to the truth sown so long ago and I rejoice and plant on.

In spite of how it sometimes feels, problems have a way of going away and growth has a way of coming. Betty Carlson, in her book *Life Is for Living*, tells of rummaging in her attic one day and coming across an old devotional book which she had used years before. As she thumbed through it she saw where she had written in the margin of one of the pages, "Never shall I forget this terrible day." But she said that as hard as she tried, she could not remember a single problem she had faced during that time, much less on that day. Whatever she was supposed to remember as long as she lived had vanished without a trace.

Problems will never completely disappear from ministry. Nor should they. If they completely disappeared we would be working where we could make no difference. A ministry without problems and problem people would not be ministry, it would be heaven, and it's far too early for most of us to show up there.

What we must do again and again is to relish the progress we do see occurring: people who are better because our lives have brushed theirs. We have to believe that what Fulton Sheen said is true, "As a baby's cry would be meaningless in a universe without a mother's love, so our restlessness with the way things are would be meaningless without the love of God" (Fulton Sheen in *The Love That Waits for You*). We have to believe that. We have to believe that people genuinely want to be better and to be changed. We have to believe that behind every obstinate heart there is, if we wait long enough, a reverse gear; that under the dullest face there is a concerned heart.

We will never take our people to heaven by ourselves. That is God's work. Our work is to lead them in the right direction. That may be tedious at times. But if we look hard enough we will discover that while we may not have taken our people nearly as far as we would like, at least we are taking them forward. Gradually we are closing the gap between them and God.

Ezekiel had seen it once and recorded it for all time. If he were looking today, he would see it hundreds of times. He would see men and women from every community hurrying to the chasms of pain and sin that threaten the life of the church. He would see bravery unparalleled in any other profession. Men who thought they possessed no courage rush to the scene and stand in the gap and close up the wall so rudely ravaged by sin. And every time they do, Satan is defeated and Christ is praised.

In a hundred unsung ways these heroes of today dare the powers of evil and stand their ground. They point men and women to Christ and then stand quietly in the shadows to ensure that their fragile souls make it safely to him. It is unlikely that the records kept in this life will ever show the full measure of their work for God, but the record is there. Somewhere in the memory bank of heaven, there must be a label which reads, "People who not only saved themselves, but a score of others as well." And if you are a pastor, no matter how great or small your church, you will be among them.

Ezekiel had sought for a man to stand in the gap and make up the hedge. When that file is opened, we will discover that Ezekiel's search succeeded. In a thousand villages that he never saw, God found a man and a gap was closed.

9

Keep Holding Up Those Hands

Celebrating Other Pastors

As a casual observer, you would never have made the connection. If you had been strolling along that afternoon through the Valley of Rephadim, you could have looked off to your right and seen two ragtag regiments clashing swords and severing heads in a full-blown battle.

Frankly, as a resident of Palestine, you would not have been too surprised. That was a routine fact of life in that region. People who lived in that landbridge between three continents had come to expect it: skirmishes, invasions, wars. If no one was fighting, they would have guessed their neighbors had died. It was one of the occupational hazards of living there, so you would have ambled on nodding your head at the sadness of the scene.

However, if you had stood long enough and looked closely enough, one feature of the fight would have captured your attention. You would have known it to be a common characteristic of battles, but never had it occurred with such abruptness. One minute one side is scoring all the hits and beating the other into a pulp. And the next instant it's the other way around. Hit and win. Run and lose. Back and forth. The scene would have furrowed your brow. What in the world could be causing such an abrupt reversal every few minutes? What made the same stroke in one instance seem to land at the neck and the next to swing wildly through the air?

It would have been puzzling and unnatural, as if the fighters were controlled by a giant hand like puppets on a string. One moment they're winning, and the next they're losing, and there's nothing on the field of battle that could possibly be making that much difference.

If you had glanced up the slope behind you, you would have seen three more observers watching the battle from the top of the hill. One of them would be quite a bit older than the other two and in his hand he would be holding a sturdy stick. You would have been baffled as to why he seemed bent on holding the stick so consistently above his head. Perhaps he was pretending that he had something to do with the battle below.

Occasionally the two younger men would point to a rock and urge the older man to sit down. And he would. But always his hands held the stick high over his head. As his arms swayed from fatigue, the two men would step to his side and grab his arms and join him in elevating the rod. It would seem like an odd way to watch a battle, almost as if the three of them were trying to reenact the lifting of the swords in the flurry of fury below. But if holding up a stick made them happy, you would hardly want to spoil their vicarious fun.

If somebody had stopped you and said, "Hey, those men up there are helping those men down there win the battle," you would have clicked off one more silly on your counter for a total of four.

But as odd as it might have seemed, there was a divine link between the men on the mountain and the battlers on the plain. In God's strategy, when the three men on the mountain pooled their strength to keep the rod raised high, their regiment in the valley prevailed. But if one of them grew tired and allowed their arms to momentarily droop, the enemy invariably turned the tide.

The winning strategy was simple. With Moses sitting on a rock between them, Aaron and Hur planted themselves by his side, locked their arms in supportive love, and together the three men hoisted the rod and struck the victory pose. It was the divine formula for unity and strength.

If one of those soldiers had glanced up from the thick of things to see those three men locked in a victory clasp, he would have surged with new enthusiasm. His leaders were pulling for him. There they stood at the top of the mountain, three hearts beating as one. The soldiers could only faintly see the rod, but there was no question about it. Moses and Aaron and Hur were firmly united behind them. If those three men were pleading with God, the victory was just a matter of time.

If the picture of Moses and Aaron and Hur could carry only one point, it must be this: we as leaders over God's people are in this together. When national figures mar the image of the ministry, we all lose a little. When unseen and unsung pastors perform their work in a spirit of sacrificial love, we all win a little. For all of our differences, we as ministers of God are bound up in the bundle of ministry together. What Dale Brown, coach at LSU, said about the team concept of his players is true for us in the ministry as well, "The best potential for me is we."

I'm like you. No matter what criteria we use to assess pastoral leadership, there are still a few of our colleagues who will always seem to us to be just plain odd, a few of them whose attic boards seem a little loose. If I had been personally recruiting people to work in the kingdom, there are a few people who would never have made my list. As one fellow put it, there will forever be, even in ministry, a few people who are the "oddly godly."

There is, for example, one dear fellow who pastors some miles from here who strikes me as the perfect cluster of human oddities. The number of things that he does differently seems to be larger than the number which he does in harmony with the rest of the pastoral race. He refuses to have a church board because he wants to call all his own shots. And I was laboring under the assumption that churches were supposed to operate with a touch of democracy. He takes off two full days a week because he says his people get two days off; why shouldn't he? And here I was assuming that one day off was plenty. He never buys Christmas presents for his wife and children because he says his people are supposed to do that. And to think I've been buying my wife a little something for nearly fifteen years. He cuts his grass on Sunday afternoon. That practice may not be a sin, but it sure gets the eyebrows up at the local drugstore, especially since he wears his standard polka-dot Bermudas and T-shirt as he sallies across his lawn.

I have long since given up trying to figure that fellow out, and I still don't have the faintest notion of why God picked him. But I celebrate him in large part because he is my favorite expression of the mysterious work of God in our world. Most of the people in his congregation think he's nearly divine. And while I feel a good deal differently, I'm happy that he's reaching a collection of people whom I will never know. When I get to heaven, one of the questions on my list has to do with why Fred got selected. But even before I get to God and raise the question, I am sure he has an answer. Probably a simple and quick one. But I still want to hear it.

Every vocation probably needs a few unlikely types just to keep us humble and to keep us guessing. But even the people whom we think of as definitely different give us reason to praise God's capacity for working with almost anything. Won't it be funny if we land in heaven and discover that we were on the "unusual specimen" list as well?

When we set about reflecting on the host of other pastors who serve along side us in the ministry, there are several directions in which our gratitude can go. Perhaps none is more needed in our day of denominational proliferation than a celebration of the enormous variety of denominations within the unity of the church. For all we say about the difference among us, there is still a great deal of unity around the essentials which we all accept and respect.

There is a tendency for people to be quick critics because there is a different church on every corner. They point to the verse about Jesus praying for his church to be one and point a wagging finger at the abomination of denominations up and down the street. The accusations may have a measure of truth, but there's a lot more going on than meets the eye. When you take the larger look, you discover that four churches per block may not so much reflect a loss of unity as it does a need for diversity within the unity. Our critics usually don't look at the deeper social needs of people. They point to the individual titles or the marquees and because they assume that competition is the name of the game, they only see the church as a sprawling mass of religious rivals bent on wiping each other out for the sake of selfishness.

But consider these position reasons for so much denominational diversity:

1. *Social Comfort Zone.* All of us have a need to find a social comfort zone. We only fool ourselves if we say that we can be equally at home with all kinds of people. That simply isn't true. And churches often develop to respond to people who fit into a particular social niche and want their worship to reflect the styles and structures of that strata as well.

I remember a university student with an independent spirit who started a house church three miles from the church to which he had belonged. When the president of the university, who lived across the street from the new house church, continued to drive the three miles to the university church, the student was peeved.Why didn't the president come to his church? Why did he need to drive right by him on the way to the church in town? By way of a response, I asked the student a couple of questions. Why did you stop attending the university church? Was three miles too far for you to drive? He replied that he had felt

out of place. I wondered out loud if perhaps the president
might have felt out of place at his house church too. For
both of them it was a matter of finding a social grouping
into which they could comfortably fit and worship.

2. *Timing Patterns.* Another reason why there is so much
diversity has to do with the matter of timing. Because of
growth or revival new groups tend to reach out into a community at different times. When the Spirit brings a surge of
growth to a denomination, it opens new doors of outreach
and inspires the church to want to reach out in fresh ways
into the community. That group might join itself to an
older established church, but the inertia of traditional patterns might stifle the fervency of the new growth, so
groups tend to start from scratch and of course in time
come to wrestle with their own traditions and inertia.

So like windblown seeds, floating over a plot of ground,
new movements are blown by the winds of the Spirit over
a community and where the soil is still barren, they find a
place to land and live. Any single plant might never be
able to cover the whole plot, but taken together the various
plants produce an erosion-preventing cover that provides
a continuous covering for the whole.

3. *Individualism.* A third factor which contributes to our
diversity is really the marriage of two assumptions: one
from the church and the other from society in general. The
idea from the church is the belief that we are a priesthood
of believers, each with his or her own unique ability to go
to God for himself. The other assumption, which is so
much a part of western society, is the steady emphasis on
individualism. Each person is a unit unto himself. His
decisions may impact others to an extreme degree, but he
is still free to pick and choose.

When these two assumptions are taken together, it is
hardly surprising that they express themselves in the
church by spawning a regular rash of offshoots. To praise
individualism in the marketplace and ridicule it in the
church is both unfair and unwise. The boundary between
these two worlds and the way they function is simply not

that sharp. What deserves our praise is the fact that for all of its reflection of individualism, denominations still demonstrate a remarkable ability to get along.

Even though the church, like all other institutions, is a participant in the individualistic spirit, its people in some deep mysterious way have a sense that they are part of a higher whole. Really when you take into account the centrifugal forces that are forever pulling us apart, it is quite a miracle that we even maintain the measure of unity that we do.

4. *Pastor.* A few people decide on a worship setting primarily because of the pastor. They like his voice, or his looks, or his style. They want a man involved in the community, or a great preacher, or a teacher type. And it is a mark of maturity to know that we won't land on everybody's island of expectations.

The data suggests that out of your congregation about 20 percent think you're God's gift to humanity; another 20 percent think you came from elsewhere; and the 60 percent in the middle are always thinking about it. They also are the ones who sway the vote. Sometimes when a person or two opens the door and walks down the street to another church, they aren't reflecting so much on you as they are indicating that they found a person whom they like a little better and who is teaching God's Word as well. But we ought not weep over that for in our clearer moments we know that they are people in our church who don't flick our switch much either. So occasionally we probably need to accept the exodus of a few people. We may not chase them away, but neither should we try to change to fit their needs. There are plenty of pastors who can nurture them equally well in the most holy faith. Perhaps we should think of it as entrusting them to a friend and fellow laborer down the street. We are in this thing together, so we should celebrate their going just as we do their coming. As we do, the larger unity which unites us stays in proper tension with the diversity that is forever threatening to divide us.

As a pastor we also add to the glory of our thoughts by

reveling in the unique strength of the people in our profession. Sometimes when I sit at my desk and gaze out the window at the other spires across town, I feel sure that God could have chosen a dozen other people who would have been better at my job than I am. The people who sit in my church have two or three areas of need that my skills don't even match. A growing number of them need professional counseling at a level far beyond my ability to give. When I talk with them, I know deep in my heart of hearts that a lot of my advice is born of the moment and is bound to be flawed. But they can't afford the sixty dollars an hour for trained advice, so I pray to God and examine the Scriptures and go at them one more time, praying all the while that the Spirit will add his wisdom to my fragmented thoughts.

Nor do I have the skills necessary to supervise the construction of a new sanctuary. We probably could use one; but while I'm here, I doubt it will happen. Not because I don't want it. But because I know that my people know that if I got one started, someone else would have to carry the weight and make the decisions and guide the task. And I'm not sure my confidence would survive that for weeks on end. So I keep the project in low profile and hope God doesn't drop a set of blueprints into my lap.

I know my deficiencies. I'm not naive about them. In fact at times I am overwhelmed by them. But what should I do? Should I leave? Should I belch out my feelings of inadequacies to my people and tell them to start looking for someone else? Should I just throw in the towel and quit?

It seems that when I struggle most with my feelings of inadequacy, one other pesky thought drops in to add to my dilemma. And that is, that all the other pastors in town are exact fits, that their skills precisely dovetail with the needs and expectations of their people. If I stay with the thought long enough, realism muscles in to help me realize that the whole bunch of us at times wrestle with the monster of inadequacy. We usually don't discuss it at our ministerial meetings because we really don't have time to delve the depths of our pain. But the other people drop enough hints, and we joke enough about our personal purgatories to let me know that I'm not the only one who sometimes asks myself, *What in the world are you doing here?*

So we leave our meetings and go back to give as much as we can to as many as we can, fully aware that the next pastor of our people may well have to fill in some serious gaps, but also aware that we are doing that right now for the person who preceded us.

Try It

In any change from one minister to another, both the incoming pastor and the people will have to make adjustments. Because each of us is different, it takes time for a church to get comfortable with a new leader, and he with them. For some people in your church the previous pastor was their favorite pastor of all time. Every person has a favorite pastor. The good news is, you will also be for some of them, *their* favorite pastor.

As you compare yourself with the previous pastor, what gaps did he leave that you are now filling? Was he a good administrator and a weak preacher, while you are just the opposite? Was he weak on visiting the people but good at motivating large groups for outreach? What are you doing now that complements what he did before?

Think ahead. What will the next pastor need to do well in order to balance out elements in your leadership style? Will he need to be a strong counselor, or a communicator, or a person who is good at pushing programs?

It is a great relief to know that, over time, God usually brings in leaders with enough gifts to meet the major needs of a people. Often it happens through a senior pastor and a staff, but if a church has only one pastor on the staff, that church can have lay leaders assume the roles, or else enjoy the ministry of various pastors who, over time, balance each other in meeting the ministry needs of the church.

At times when you feel unqualified and unworthy for your task, you might want to reflect on another pastor whom you know who lacks about every skill in the book, but is still enjoying a measure of success in his ministry.

I usually think of Gordon. He pastors in a tiny, white clapboard church in North Dakota. The people who attend his church are honest about him. "His knowledge of the Bible," they say, "is pretty sparse. In fact when he preaches you get more fire than wood."

Gordon never went beyond the sixth grade in school, but that doesn't keep him from trying and caring. I have never praised ignorance, but in Gordon's case—and with his training—I am convinced that God likes what he sees when Gordon gets up to preach. His preaching is best known for its detours. At least a dozen times per sermon he uses the line, "Now this is probably a little off the subject." He could leave out the "little." Even his prayers have three or four minisermons embedded in them, but hardly anybody listens to Gordon because of his focus or because of his notes. They listen because of his spirit. When he preaches, there is something finer about the man than anything he ever says. For this time and for that place, Gordon is the right man for the job.

When we take the long view on our work, and when we remember people like Gordon whom God is using so powerully, we remind ourselves again in the profoundest way that God is the one who makes our ministry. He is the one who takes our paltry gift and multiplies it for the feeding of the crowd. We can't do *everything*—but we can do *something*. And our unique set of gifts might well be exactly what God wants at our place for this time.

In our dog-eat-dog world there is also reason to celebrate when among our churches the spirit of cooperation overtakes and stifles the spirit of competition. When Jesus prayed that his followers be one, he didn't need to mention the spirit of competition that our western world would foster twenty centuries later. His world knew nothing of market shares and goldfish effects and bigger-is-better business tactics. The world into which he thrust his disciples had very few spiritual enterprises that even came close to the life-changing message he was proclaiming, and those were scattered so widely that they rarely bumped on competitive terms. There were plenty of movements vying for people's loyalty, but most of them were so pervasively pagan that Christianity had an easy time being perceived as unique.

But since the time of Christ, Christianity has spawned over seventy thousand separate bodies, some as large as the Roman Catholic Church and others as small as an independent house church. And alongside the burgeoning number of organizations, there has also been a major emergence of competition. Businesses prey on their neighbors and churches are doing it too. Brokers are vying for new dollars. And the media spars on the airwaves. With all the cutthroat politics going on around us, it is not impossible for a measure of competition to creep into the soul of the church. The tendency for us to compare churches on the basis of numbers is only one more symptom that the world is very much with us.

But when Christ prayed for unity, perhaps his farsighted mind could envision the day when his churches would sit four to an intersection, all claiming to be pointing to the true way. Perhaps he knew that what we would need in the twentieth century was not the grace to endure persecution from without, but grace to endure comparison from within. He knew that competition would cause too many of his followers to form a firing squad and line up in a circle facing each other. He knew that the degrees of difference between us would be small—the distinguishing features fairly negligible. So he mentioned the need for unity.

He knew we would have competition; but he wanted us to remember that we would have enough from Satan and sin without adding to our enemies from within. The last thing he wanted was for us to be at odds with people on our own team. It was a prayer of enormous foresight that we fulfill every time we celebrate our fellow pastors. We may never agree on all the details, but that should only hint to us, not of the narrowness of people but of the great-

ness of God. In his majesty he is able to join all our tiny
boundaries into his eternal boundary and include far more
people in his kingdom than any single denomination could
ever be able to do on its own. We may feel that certain
denominations fall short in clearly directing people toward
God, but until we are able to muster a force to draw a map
for every single person, we do well to celebrate the sketchy
diagrams. They are far better than no map at all.

Sometimes in a selfish moment we resent another pastor
who looks like he is about to wedge a little deeper into our
share of the market. We see him two doors down the street
from our church, talking to people whom we are sure
ought to be in our church, and we scowl at his brazen
boldness. But we can smother that resentment by calling to
mind again one simple truth: churches never draw their
people from a neatly boundaried territory. Church con-
stituencies are the epitome of social osmosis. Baptists and
Methodists and Quakers and Episcopalians live side by
side up and down our streets. They even rib each other
about their different denominations, and enjoy it. But then
on Sundays they go four separate ways to worship. And
that is great. Worship is such a highly personal matter and
such a lofty event that most of us are comfortable with
only one or two worship styles. Most of us feel rather
strongly about how we should approach God. For several
of my neighbors the raucous celebration of God at one
church in our town with all its hollering and yelling is a
version of blasphemy. But for another neighbor the reading
of a homily from a desk perched high above the audience
with incense wafting through the air is a formal ritual as
dead as a graveyard.

Frankly I harbor no hope of ever bringing these two
neighbors together in one sanctuary, nor do I really care to.
They both are reflecting a very sound principle—worship
styles should match our personal preference.

The ways of a heart to God are as multifaceted as the
ways of a woman to a man. Like the selection of a spouse,
the selection of a worship setting is nothing to be dealt

with glibly. We're talking the future of our souls. We must make sure that the site we select to meet with God is a place where we can be fully and happily at home.

Nobody in their right mind ever started looking for a spouse with the attitude, "Hey, I'll take the first thing that walks through the door. A spouse is a spouse after all. What does it matter what she [or he] looks like, or how he [or she] thinks or how that person behaves? My commitment is to marriage, not to any particular person." No reasonable person ever says that. Worship follows a similar pattern. No thinking person ever says, "I want to get to God. I don't really care what worship style I use. All of them are about the same anyway. Just put me anywhere, and I'll be right at home. After all, I'm into God, not how you approach him."

We don't say that. And shouldn't. If we did, we would need to question our own seriousness about the importance of genuine worship. If any way to God is okay with us, we're overlooking the highly intense and personal nature of worship. We should make it a point to choose carefully the feeding place of our soul. And happily, our world provides a number of venues from which to choose.

So I celebrate both my neighbors: the one who likes the rafters to shake and the one who likes the rafters to smell. Their pastors are doing what I'm doing. They are leading their own group of people as near to God as their unique avenues of personality will allow. And they are like me too in this one frustration: they discover that even if their style strongly suits their people's needs, they still have a few who fail to take full advantage of the atmosphere of mystery to get closer to God.

When I smart a bit from the fact that my fellow pastor drives his bus right to the steps of my church to pick up people for a trip across town, I must remind myself that he is not my competitor but my colleague. We're after the same thing and pursuing the same goal. Perhaps there are people at his church steps that I should be pursuing because they would never think of worshiping with him. When he picks up my people by my church, he's working for me. Maybe I need to be working a little harder for him. We struggle with jealousy when we forget that we are working, not to build our church, but *his* church; that as pastors we are not marshaled against each other, but rather standing back-to-back against the onslaught of sin.

I haven't always felt that way. I remember as a twenty year-old the shock of attending my first community ministerial meeting. It started with the clothing. I had been to my own denominational ministerial meetings where every pastor looked alike: two-piece dark suits with subdued ties, dark, well-shined shoes, and a close-cropped haircut. They looked like they had been cloned and then sent by the shoe-shine booth on their way to the parsonage. It was a study of solids in sequence, a set of duplicates so neat and well-defined, they looked exactly like they had come all in one batch from the copy machine. And I was proud of their uniformity. I thought that was the only way a group of real pastors should look.

And then I went to my first ministerial—and the assembly line had broken down. The men and women sitting around that table were not exactly cut from the same cloth. And they certainly hadn't shopped at the same clothier. I had heard of clerical collars, but I had never seen that many in one place. My first thought was to wish I could wear one. But I remembered a friend who warned me to be suspicious of people who needed a choker to let you know they were in the ministry. So I fought the thought. Plus their gray cloaks seemed awfully formal, so I wrote them off as unsavory thieves. They probably drove Porsches and gave a ten-minute homily filled with pablum and then luxuriated the rest of the week in Palm Beach. So I disdained those "arrogant" types and felt strongly impressed by God to keep a cool distance from them. After all, they were smug swindlers, and what better place for God to give them a lesson in humility than right there in the icy company of us holier ones. I was only twenty, but at least I had come from the correct company, and what little my age and wisdom could contribute, I certainly wanted to willingly give.

Then there were women in the group. I had met a few women pastors in my time, but these women sat there wearing cheery, bright colors which looked more like a flower garden in springtime than the drab dull colors I knew really belonged on a woman who claimed a call. When I shook my head in dismay, I always tried to be looking away from them so they wouldn't think I was being disrespectful. But in my heart I knew that if they ever really met God on the Damascus Road, they would do away with all those flowery colors and earthy tones and fade back into the drab gray and blue I had seen on my assembly line.

But the fellow who really set me back was the chap in the Hawaiian shirt. At first I thought he must be a guest of one of the other ministers who was into friendship evangelism. But the more he talked, the more I feared that he was one of us. His shirt was open three buttons down and on his chest hung the gaudiest pendant I had ever seen. It was about the size of a wrecking ball and about as gold as the Dome of the Rock. Every time he leaned forward to make a point, that globe would come pouring out of his shirt, shearing off a few more of his black chest hairs in the swing. During the meeting I moved my salvation scope as far up and down the scale as I could, and I never could see how he could be a Christian, much less a minister. If he was in midlife crisis, that was one thing, but to claim to be working for God was pure sacrilege. Whatever side he took on a vote, I took the other. I hadn't thought through all the issues we were voting on, but I knew I couldn't go wrong if I just made sure he was on the opposite side. I could hardly wait to get out of there and back with God's people. I needed to breathe divine air again, and until I could, I vowed to hold my breath. None of the stale stuff from this room was going to get in my lungs. If these were the pastors of our community, I shivered to think what their congregations must look like. Especially the people who sat in front of that man with the half-buttoned shirt.

I truly believe that all beginning pastors need to go through a time of clarifying their identity in the ministry. They need to pass, even if briefly, through a time when they feel that their way of knowing God is the best way, if not the only way. They need to know their niche. Perhaps they could never truly know where to fit into the plan of redemption unless they have passed through a phase when they were sure that their view of God was the only way God wanted to be viewed. There is a confidence that comes with such certainty that probably could never be gained in any other way.

As a pastor's confidence and identity comes more clearly into focus, he is also able to relinquish his monopoly on the truth and allow himself the privilege of looking at the way another dedicated person is viewing the same God. A few persons fixate in the narrow phase and become victims of their own box. They often go for years incarcerated in a cell of infallibility. Their narrow definition of God not only forces them to overemphasize one feature of his grand person, but also to lose out on so many other virtues of him that they can never know because they were afraid to look. Instead of being celebrants they become censors. Instead of reveling in the panoramic beauty of his person, they zero in on one tiny peephole and fall into the heresy of hideboundness.

As scary as it can be at first, it is absolutely essential for us as pastors and leaders to widen our wonder. If God is so great that the heaven of heavens cannot contain him, then he must also be great enough to work with people in ways that do not fully fit inside our personal preferences. When we reduce his will to a kind of clothing or the size of a necklace, we have whittled him down far smaller than a God his size is able to go. It is true that God loves us as if there wasn't anybody else to love, but that's the way he loves that pendant pastor too. And the women in the red and pink. And the starchy-collared crew.

I don't exactly remember when I moved away from criticism to admiration for my colleagues in ministry. Perhaps God brought the change gradually so I wouldn't feel such a shock to my pride. Perhaps he led me along the slow way because he knew I would react if he told me the truth about my Pharisaism all at once. At twenty I was in no frame of mind to think that any other way but my way was the right way. For that time it was perhaps the only thing I could do, but with the passing of the years I have come an amazingly long way. I would not blot out the memory of my rigidity for anything; it helps me understand a lot of others who are dealing with the same dilemma I faced. But neither would I for a million bucks go back. I still don't agree with all the emphases of the pastors who work around me. I still think some of them are missing the gate and hitting the fence. But I also am more and more convinced that all the statements I have made in the pulpit are not the sum and substance of divinity either. I am aiming as high as my limited mind can reach. I am trying to explain Christ and his message of redemption as clearly as my awkward mind can do. But I am more and more aware of the yawning gap between my reach and his reality.

Try It

On the inside back cover of this book make a list of a half-dozen or so assumptions that you used to hold which you have now discarded. What are some of the ideas you held onto at the beginning of your ministry that you would be embarrassed to believe today? If you take the time to write them down, you will probably find yourself a bit uncomfortable just reducing them to print. You'd certainly hate it if anybody found them unless they were clearly labeled: THINGS I USED TO BELIEVE.

As you think about the list, what was it that caused you to change your position on this or that? Was part of your problem in the beginning a lack of knowledge? A prejudice you learned from other people? An interpretation of the Bible which you have since changed?

Is it possible to start out mature enough not to have to change much (if anything) in our beliefs? Do you know any fellow pastors who have refused to grow with themselves?

In my county, there are twenty-two churches which belong to my denomination. At times the competition overshadows the cooperation. Three of the churches are especially strong rivals. Several gossipmongers in town have taken it as their personal burden to stake out the three churches in order to spread around the latest on the turf wars.

It came as a surprise one Sunday when a new pastor to one of the churches spent his whole pastoral prayer begging God's help for the other twenty-one churches around the county. A few of his faithful were sure he had misplaced his mind. Several predicted an immediate exodus to all the other churches that he had praised so highly. It never came. Instead the church grew. A spirit of cooperation wedged in to replace the spirit of friction. At one point two of the pastors even talked of merger. Five years earlier that would have been the height of heresy.

There's probably not a pastor alive who hasn't at one time or another wondered how it would be to pastor another group of people. You may not have let the thought get out of hand and grow into covetousness, but at least you've entertained it for a while. *If I could just get a church like that one*, runs the illogic, *I could really make a difference. If I didn't have to deal with a power-hungry board, I could grow a great church too.* It's amazing how shallow our thinking gets when it leaves reality and glides over into fantasy. All of a sudden we are able to trim away the problems, play up the glory, and before you know it every church in the community looks like it's sitting on greener grass than yours. It's only in our saner moments that we remember that most greener grass grows over septic tanks!

A quick look around is all you need to see that the battle against sin is going against us. Here and there a group of Christians are advancing, but in the larger grid, the points of regression are often outnumbering the points of growth. In a situation like ours, it's no time to be ridiculing each other and arguing over who has the best place. If the lines are to be pushed back and Satan's kingdom diminished, every soldier, no matter how weak or wounded, is needed on the line. The fact that Christ promised to build his church doesn't make anything automatic. The tension is very much with us; the array on the opposing side is still visible and strong.

Reinforcement is the order of the day. Every chance we have to affirm our fellow soldiers is one more chance to rout the real competitor. Every hand we can lift is one more hand to help halt the advance of the enemy. When we grasp the full seriousness of the battle in which we are engaged, we always bypass the quibbling about carpets and colors and clothes and churches. We do with what we have and go forward, trusting that all up and down the line our fellow soldiers will do the same. In fact if we can keep the front line solid, who knows how far we can push the enemy back?

As we clasp hands with our neighbors and hold their hands high in conquest, we will discover that our arms are less weary, not only because of the support of our arched arms, but also because God has joined in our grip and is bearing most of the weight from above.

10

The Just Shall Live by Faith

Celebrating a Faith that Endures

Habakkuk was discouraged. He had preached his heart out to the same people for ten years and as far as he could tell, they were about where they were when he started. The complaints were still outnumbering the commitments and unfairness was building walls of hatred among his people. He had seen a few advances, but when he drew a line and added up the score, sin and obedience were in a dead heat. For every step of progress, his people had taken another step back. It was a frustrating fight and Habakkuk was at wit's end to know what to do about it. He had tried to mold his people in holy habits and guide them in the ways of peace, but the things he thought he had finally gotten nailed down in their lives kept coming loose.

One day, as he was venting his frustration to God, he got a stunning response. He had prayed for help, for something to break the cycle of sin, but what God had in mind took him totally by surprise. He was not naive about the severity of his people's sin, but the solution seemed so shocking that it took him aback: the Babylonians would be coming.

Habakkuk had heard about that group. They lived across the mountains to the east in the Tigris Valley, and almost nothing friendly ever came from over there. In fact the rumor was that the Babylonians didn't just kill; they tortured. As Habakkuk glanced at the range of mountains to the east, he shuddered at the thought of Babylonians cresting the top of that ridge with their horses and chariots and unrelenting spears. No matter how fully they prepared, the people of Israel would be little more than sitting ducks. The struggle would be over in a flash.

The more he thought on it, the more Habakkuk wrestled with an inner tug of war. He knew that his people had sinned, and that God could not tolerate their behavior forever, but it seemed odd to him that God would replace one group of sinners with another—just a larger bunch of the same. The Babylonians were no saints! So what could one bad bunch pummeling another bad bunch really accomplish?

When he mentioned it to God, the answer came back with two great insights. "Habakkuk," God said, "I know about Babylon. I know about their sins and their atrocities. And even though they will visit Israel in judgment, their own days are numbered as well. Don't worry, Habakkuk, I'm not missing anything.

"But, Habakkuk," God continued, "there's something I need to remind you of personally. You've gotten bogged down in discouragement and it's hard for you to see the long view. It's hard for you to see any solution to this predicament that you and your people are in. But Habakkuk, when things get gloomy, and celebration is the furthest thing from your mind, there's one thing that circumstances can never take away from you—one sure grip in this downstream world. Habakkuk, when things are going terribly wrong and you can't find a solitary place to rest and refresh your soul, you've got to remember your faith. Nobody can take away your faith. They may ridicule you to your face, and flaunt their sins, and laugh at your calls for righteousness, but nobody—neither your enemies from without nor your critics from within—can yank away your faith. And Habakkuk, I want to remind you of what I have been telling my people since the dawn of history: the righteous keep living by faith. That goes for prophets too. Prophets are marvelous people, but there are times when the only thing they can know for sure is that their faith is firmly fixed, that they have made a decision to believe in me no matter what. I'll probably be saying this to you several times to make sure you believe it again deeply, but Habakkuk, never, *never* forget it. Righteous people live from the inside out for righteous people live by faith."

The rule has been on the books since the Garden of Eden and pastors are not exempt; we too earn our living by the sweat of our brow. Translated into pastoral language, that means that we will never get beyond the strain and drain in our lives. The same feelings of routine and drudgery which occasionally mark the lives of our people will at times mark ours as well.

Every pastor goes through periods in his work when the last thing he wants to do is celebrate. The angry barbs of criticism are gouging so deeply into his heart that about all he can do is flinch and back away. Rarely do people know how deeply they hurt a man with a sensitive heart. Many of them are probably used to cutthroat tactics in their world of work. Many of them function in a work environment in which aggression is the rule of thumb. But churches aren't meant to work that way, and the pastor who has been trying to manage with gentleness is often the victim of a technique that is foreign to his heart. Often the venom numbs or even kills a portion of his soul. It can take months and even years to rally fully from a heavy round of hatred.

To say that it is possible to keep a happy, upbeat face in the middle of such agony is naive. When outer circumstances turn bitter and sour, the face can't help but reflect a measure of the stress. The happy edge can't help but be dulled. Being fully human we know quite well the many moods of ministry and despair belongs in the bunch.

In times like that when the soul is staggering under the weight of pain, there really is only one sure hope: our solid belief in God. We have preached with power that God could help an Athanasius as he stood against the world. We have spoken with confidence about a God who could help John Bunyan write *Grace Abounding* while deteriorating in a prison. And suddenly the wheel has rolled around, and it's our turn to show the reliability of God—to show that when all outer hope is gone, there is a steady, confident hope which resides in the heart and which dares to believe in spite of the pain.

Thankfully for most of us, the wheel doesn't rest on one space forever. In his unique way, God knows when to bring relief and break the deadlock and move us back into a more enjoyable phrase. The days of our difficulty may, as they did for Habakkuk, seem eternal, but they are also numbered. God honors our faith and with his uncanny sense of timing offers seasons of relief.

In his grand design there is never a single, horrible memory but what God plans to eclipse it with a better one. It may not be blotted out completely, but it certainly will recede. Like green grass sprouting to recolor a burned-over field, so God brings along beauty for ashes, and a garment of praise for the spirit of heaviness.

As a guest minister to a church in another state, I remember one Sunday afternoon sitting alone in the pastor's study at the church when I heard a knock at the door. The man who stood at the entrance looked to be about seventy years old. A small scrap of gray hair hung down over his weathered forehead, and his hands were gnarled and worn. He introduced himself as John, and asked me if he could share a brief story. I had made a hobby out of gathering beautiful stories from older saints, and John seemed to fit the mold. Little did I know that his would be one of the most gripping stories I would ever hear, and one to which I would often return in memory when times were bad.

John sat down in a rocker about ten feet away and shared his story. "Pastor," he began, "I heard you mention in your sermon this morning about your rough home life as a child, and I wanted to tell you a little about mine. I've shared it with people as a means of encouragement. Maybe it will help you deal with your memories a little better too.

"I was born into a family of twelve children. My father worked on the railroad and to my knowledge I never remember him eating a meal with the family while I was home. I was the youngest of the twelve children, and the few dollars he scraped together from his salary and a few odd jobs simply didn't make ends meet. The money problems were so bad that the family lived under constant strain.

"Finally my dad ran off with another woman leaving mother to care for all twelve children and with no income. It was the lowest point in our lives. One day when I was six years old, my mother took me on her knee, and I noticed she was crying. She said, 'Son, I love you very much, but unless I let someone else adopt you, you will probably starve to death. I simply can't keep you here. I plan to put you and three of your sisters up for adoption.'

"The next week, pastor, she placed an ad in the newspaper of a nearby town and within three days a couple got in touch. I remember the day my mother took me to the train station to send me off forever to my new home. She cried all the way to the depot. I was only six, but because mother was crying, I cried too. I didn't fully understand what was happening. I did not know that I would never see my mother again. But I had a gnawing feeling in my little heart that whatever was happening, it was terribly final and sad. It was the worst feeling I have ever had in my life.

"When the train finally stopped and the doors opened for me to leave, my mother never told me good-bye. She couldn't. She was crying out loud now. All she could do was kneel down and hug me like she had never hugged me before. It was a long tear-stained hug like someone had just died.

"Pastor, when the conductor reached down and took me from my mother's arms, I felt something die on the inside, and till this day there's a part of me that is completely gone, dead, buried. I glanced at my mother once out the window of the train as it pulled away and I never saw her again.

"My new family was lovely, and took good care of me, but it never was the same anymore. Nothing they could do ever overcame the pain that I had experienced that day at the depot. I had been abandoned. The rip had opened such a gaping wound in my heart that I doubted if it would ever be healed. I went for years unable to accept my adoptive parents much less respond to their incredible love.

"In a few years I grew into adulthood and went out on my own. I spent year after year absorbing myself with my work, trying to bury the chasm in my soul. But one day something beautiful happened. In a moment of great discouragement I visited a church in the town where I was working, hoping that I might hear a word that would boost my spirits. To my amazement the preacher that morning spent the whole sermon talking about how God loves to adopt people. When he asked if there was anybody who would like to join God's family, I took him up and went forward. As I knelt there, I remembered the train and the depot and my mother's tears when I had glanced at her that last time out the window. But I also had another strong feeling that day. As I stood there Christ seemed to say, 'John, that day your mother left you, I took you into my family. That very day I sat down beside you on the train.' So that day in the church I gave Jesus my life as my way of saying thank you. And all of a sudden I felt I belonged to a real family again. I had been adopted by Jesus.

"When I think back on my life, there are two days that stand out way above the others. One is the day at the depot, and the other is the day I met Jesus. I'm sitting here with you in this study today, pastor, because Jesus took me in. And I'm happy now. After years of turmoil and hate, Jesus adopted me. I wouldn't take anything in the world for the privilege of belonging to his family because from what I heard, he'll never run low on food and have to send me away."

Before John left that afternoon, I had him pray with me. He put that gnarled hand on my head and gave thanks that the both of us had been adopted by Jesus. As I watched him disappear down the road, my whole body shivered from the power of that visit. That day I had shared with an angel from God.

Since that day, when the pressures of my work have weighed down heavily upon me and my nights are splattered with the tension of my days, I remember John and his Jesus, and the day he laid that hand on my head and joined me in celebrating our adoption by Jesus. The memory reminds me of my sonship, and I go in the strength of it for many days.

What we tend to forget in our downtimes is that even then we are doing good. By enduring under pressure and holding firm to our faith, we are delivering one of our most eloquent sermons. It would probably shock us if we could know how many people are helped when we hurt. Because of what we've gone through, many of them will succeed much better and keep Christ much closer to the center of their lives.

Ministry is such a majestic enterprise. On the one hand it has a grandeur and mystery that envelops us with amazement. On the other hand there are times when we feel thoroughly overwhelmed with the whole thing. The number of component parts in the work of the ministry could easily justify a dozen specialists, but they fall to one man who barely feels competent in one area, let alone in ten. Ministry crosses into business just enough to balance the books and pay the bills—but it never lives or dies by a balance sheet. It is bigger than that. It dips into management in order to make smart decisions in the care of people. But it is more than management. Once the help has been assigned and the strategic planning done, it leaves matters of management behind and moves on to other purposes. Ministry also borrows from the field of sociology.

Any congregation that thrives has to be committed to a dynamic body life in which the people prompt each other to winsome love. But ministry is more than bringing about social cohesion. It includes that but it is always much more.

Ministry is modeling. It means living and behaving in such a way that every life you brush will be a bit more ready for heaven because of you. It means balancing the budget. But greater, it means living a life of giving. It means cheerfully doing your part to carry the congregation forward. It means hiring and firing and making painful decisions that cause pockets of pain. But ministry also means living the truth in such a way that believers are kept on track and unbelievers have a clear sense of the error of their ways. Ministry means juggling a motley assortment of personality types and making judgments on how to weld them all together. But ministry also means living in such a way that your people know that you want them to be both—both unique and unified. It means affirming their distinctive personalities as part of the larger plan for a comprehensive ministry.

Ministry means leading by living. Every bit of belief and behavior counts. Your attitude in the board meeting is remembered when you preach. Your poise in a crisis heightens the integrity of your prayers. Everything is of a piece. Your home, your car, your office, your shopping mart—all are but miniature stages on which you are trying to show your people what a holy life looks like. If you do well in the detail, you will do well, for ministry is nothing more nor less than wholesome, integrated living under the lordship of Christ. When that truly happens, you don't need to talk as much. What you say by your life will speak so clearly the first time that when you do speak from the podium, your people will mistake it for an echo.

There's a claim abroad that the pastor of today has lost credibility in our world, that he doesn't carry the authority that he used to. That's not true. There are more pastors who mess up these days in part because there are more pastors to mess up. But the men and women who are discharging their duty with excellence of spirit and integrity of heart are creating for themselves and for God as large a pool of credibility as ever before. This is no time for us to discard our calling as a useless relic of the past, fit only for a few stained-glassed buildings, filled with antiquated pews. It's no time to sneer at our vocation and second-guess ourselves about ever having come this way. No matter how low you may feel at any given moment, there is not a single place where you minister but that you are a powerful help to somebody. There is no work that is ever useless if it is performed for the praise of God.

As pastors we deal in nonnegotiable divine tender. Our daily assignments have us dealing in dreams and memories and hopes and contentment and joy. And they are such delicate things. When they are properly ordered, our people are able to soar to the heavens but when they go awry, their worlds come tumbling down. And then we have to remind them of what God has reminded us: the righteous ones live by faith. So Sunday after Sunday we stand and say a good word for Jesus and tell our people that in spite of the odds, they still have God. Little do they know that we often preach the sermon for ourselves and hope that they will benefit from it while we're talking. If they don't, at least we know it helped the person behind the pulpit.

One of our favorite times as pastor is that lovely lull following the Sunday evening service. Our harder work of the week is finished and for a few hours, next Sunday seems miles away. We have checked the doors of the church one last time to make sure they are locked. We have switched off the last set of lights and closed one more door behind us. The church that sheltered people all day now sits solitary and lonely. We step across the yard toward home, feeling the satisfaction of having worked hard for God all day.

For just a while, as we settle into a chair and converse with friends or family, the church and its weight and worry seems far, far away, its bills and business a distant rumble in the past. For a while, our care level can drop down to a lower intensity as our sense of our own need for restoration rises to the fore.

Probably no one else could ever look at us on Sunday evening and know the depth of our joy at being able to drop into a chair and relax without having to mull over one more verse or dig out one more point. For the pastor, it's a minivacation made all the more beautiful because we have worked hard enough to deserve it. For a few hours, Sunday turns into a true Sabbath, an oasis of rest. It is one of God's most special rewards for his servants. And to the pastor who has felt the strain of a Sunday, it is a savory moment indeed.

As the fatigue of a long day gives way to the joy of rest, a lot of the headaches begin to recede and the achievements move closer and closer to the front. Two or three dark blots on a day have a way of eclipsing the sunshine. But in the quiet of a Sunday evening, with the cares of your work as far away in time as they ever get, God restores the balance and shrinks the problems down to their proper size. The longer you sit, the stronger it comes back into focus; ministry, for all its headaches and heartaches, is still the place to be. It is such a lofty calling that we would hardly expect it to come free of charge, a work with neither agony nor pain. And if it did, we likely wouldn't stick to it because nothing great would be at stake.

As it turns out, plenty is at stake and the longer we reflect on it, the more we are convinced that with all of its downside, it is the highest place we could be; that now is one of the best times of our lives; that God has put us to the plows with our heads facing forward and in his power we aim to keep on.

Over the summer our family visited Disney World in Orlando, Florida. For two days we rode and watched and visited and sampled everything in the park. We climbed the Swiss family treehouse and flew in Dumbo's Flying Circus. We bought balloons from Donald Duck and ate enough cotton candy to cause a cavity within the hour. And at the end of the two days we were beat. Our minds were brimming with memories of new adventures, but our legs had turned to rubber. When we collapsed into the car to head home, it felt like the best ride of the day.

But on the way home, we talked about our visit and decided to make a list of all the amusements and rides we had visited. As the list ballooned, we grew even more tired. No wonder we were leaning on each other at the end of the day. We had been around to twenty-one activities and five of the rides we had ridden twice. Only one ride had three little hash marks by it—The Carousel of Progress. It's that show that sits over in the corner of the park. No long lines. Nothing there that would make the major promo piece. But among the sights to see at Disney World, it rates with the best of them for having a short, sharp message which lingers in the mind long after the car has been unpacked and the souvenirs lost.

The Carousel of Progress is a circular set of seats which rotates around a giant circular stage. The stage is divided into segments that depict in sequence the progress of science over the past several decades. In each portrayal, an animated man sits at the table with an old dog lying at his feet. The man points out the latest gadgets of his generation which make for comfort in life. As the stage progresses, he talks about wringer-washers and telephones and stereos and powered painting tools and finally microwaves—dozens of inventions are highlighted in the scenes.

However, it's the *music* that dominates every scene and bridges between them that keeps pulsing in your mind. At every scene and all in between the refrain keeps running, "Now is the time, now is the best time, now is the best time of your life. . . ." At one point the man even invites the audience to join with him in singing, "Now is the time, now is the best time, now is the best time of your life. . . ."

It's a message that ought to be recorded and sent to every pastor in the world. Since we can't live in the future nor retreat to the past, we should give ourselves to the good habit of fully occupying the present, brimming instant. As important as it may be, now is still the best time of our lives. Even if we plan to leave our present assignment in six weeks, we still can search out the moments of beauty in that six weeks and live vigorously in them. Wishing time away will not make the future better. Accepting and celebrating the present helps create a habit of joy that will play well now and help us set a tone of expectation for the future.

You could hardly find a more pointed and positive parable for describing our ministry. We too are on The Carousel of Progress. Now is the best time for us too. At every stage of progress on that ride, even when the man was singing "Now is the best time," you knew that something better was coming. In just a few seconds the giant stands would move to a more advanced level of living and the song would sound out again, "Now is the time, now is the best time, now is the best time of your life."

No ministry is ever absolutely ideal. Sin is too rampant, and people are too human for that. As a matter of fact, as long as this world stands, ministry will never be ideal. There will never be a time when all our people are doing all the right things at all the right times. Every upside will always have its downside, every win a loss.

Whatever comes our way, whether a calamity as ominous as the Babylonians or an oasis as lovely as a Sunday evening right before two weeks of vacation, our greatest point of celebration must always come from the fact that in all our comings and goings, our sadness and gladness, our joys and our sorrows, we are eternally committed to living for Christ, because when all is said and done, God's people above everything else are people who live by faith.

By the eye of faith we will always be looking to model on earth the celebration that is already begun in heaven. Our work on earth is so demanding that we can only catch the celebration now in bits and pieces—but we know it's begun. When we have finished our work here, we have the sure confidence that the celebrants will throw wide the higher doors and welcome us there.

For further information or comment:
Dr. Joseph Seaborn II
Professor, Indiana Wesleyan University
4102 S. Washington Street
Marion, Indiana 46953

Phone (317) 674-6901 Ext. 246